SELF LOVED

Self Loved

A MONTH OF MEDITATIONS

Anna Fable

Copyright © 2023 by Anna Fable

All rights reserved. No part of this book may be reproduced in any manner whatsoever without written permission except in the case of brief quotations embodied in critical articles and reviews.

First Printing, 2023

Dedication

For my mother.
Who gave me the courage to love myself.

Contents

Dedication   v
Introduction   ix

The First Day   1
The Second Day   4
The Third Day   9
The Fourth Day   14
The Fifth Day   20
The Sixth Day   24
The Seventh Day   29
The Eighth Day   36
The Ninth Day   40
The Tenth Day   43
The Eleventh Day   48
The Twelfth Day   52
The Thirteenth Day   56

The Fourteenth Day	62
The Fifteenth Day	65
The Sixteenth Day	69
The Seventeenth Day	72
The Eighteenth Day	76
The Nineteenth Day	79
The Twentieth Day	83
The Twenty-First Day	87
The Twenty-Second Day	94
The Twenty-Third Day	100
The Twenty-Fourth Day	105
The Twenty-Fifth Day	107
The Twenty-Sixth Day	112
The Twenty-Seventh Day	117
The Twenty-Eighth Day	122
The Twenty-Ninth Day	128
The Thirtieth Day	133
The Author	139

Introduction

Meditation is one of the most powerful healing practices that we can employ in our lives. I have seen the effects of it firsthand, and I believe, with all my heart, that it can and will change your life. If you struggle to accept yourself and constantly fight unwanted thoughts, but meditation has always seemed out of reach, this book is here to help guide you through a 30-day meditation practice. Every day we will meditate together to develop a routine of self-compassion and serenity. We will also share affirmations and intentions to help expand these healing messages into the rest of your day.

Self-love is not a noun. It is a verb. We must *do* it. Practice it. If we don't practice self-love, it will atrophy. We can always find reasons to judge ourselves, to dislike, or even, in the worst of cases, to hate ourselves. The only way to combat this is by instituting a practice of self-compassion.

My intention for this book is to provide you with the tools to begin your practice. Once we are finished, you will have the resources to shepherd this practice into your daily life.

I wish to help anyone who is willing to help themselves—to empower you to journey into your inner world and come back filled with a complex but profound love for yourself. To carve a path of self-love and find a way back home.

Meditation:

I will be guiding you through these meditations using written words. My intention is for you to read each paragraph, engage in the exercises, and follow the instructions I offer.

Throughout the book, I will be using this symbol:

∞

This symbol indicates it's time to close your eyes and sit in the presence of your experience for as long as you are comfortable. This can be a few seconds or thirty minutes. Where you are in your journey will dictate the shape of your practice.

*Feel free to set a timer if you prefer a time limit for your meditations. Simply begin the timer whenever you see this symbol:

∞

*If words like "surrender to the present moment" don't resonate, just allow them to sit in your conscious mind and see if they slowly reveal themselves to you. Rest assured, most of us didn't know what these meant, what they felt like, or how to practice them when we started. The common thread between all of us walking the path is that we took the first step.

Setting Our Intention for These Thirty Days:

Let's take a moment to remember the reason we are doing this. We might be engaging in this practice with the intention to heal, to improve, to explore, and to inquire. We might be here to seek and to find, or to become happier, healthier, wiser, or better. I urge you to reflect on your *why*. Why have you decided to embark on this practice?

Whatever the reason, we are here. We are showing up for ourselves. We are taking time for ourselves. To be with ourselves. This is the greatest act of love. To be present. To give our presence.

As you practice presence, I urge you to recognize the gift you bestow upon yourself. When you are present with yourself, you are engaging in the act of love. You are loving yourself. It may not feel this way, but as we continue to practice, you may witness a gentleness arising within you, a kind of affection for yourself. For your struggles, for your pain, and for everything underneath all of that too. For the *you* beneath all of your experience.

I have seen meditation give birth to self-love every time it is practiced. As we look deeper, we see our worthiness of love and affection more clearly. As we peel back the layers of our understanding, we arrive at a place of acceptance for our shared humanity. We begin to recognize that, at our core, we are all made of the same stuff, and we all deserve love and kindness.

The First Day

Welcome to your first day of practice. It's an honor to connect with you, through time, through space. Thank you for sharing this practice with me.

Let's begin.

Wherever you are, whatever position your physical body is in, take a moment to bring awareness to whatever is beneath you, holding you up. What is supporting you, holding you? This point is crucial as a touchstone for the practice of understanding support. There are energies all around you, rooting for you. These energies want the best for you. They want you to succeed. If we can begin to connect with these energies, they can serve as a reminder of our worth. They are great teachers; all we need to do is learn how to listen. So, let's do just that. Gently invite your attention to the space where your body makes contact with whatever is holding you up.

Sit with this. Allow the sensation here to float in your awareness.

You may find a buzzing sensation. Or heat? Perhaps you notice tingling or something else. Something more. This sensation, whatever it is, is your life force energy. It is floating in and through you. Allow yourself to feel it. Fully. Take a moment to track your own life flowing through your physical form.

What have you noticed here? Is there anything present that you weren't aware of before you brought your attention to it? We might have bumped up against the aches and pains of living, and yet you may find something underneath all of that. Your body. Your own body, keeping you alive. Breathing life into your lungs, pumping life through your veins. Your own body believes you are worthy of this one great gift. You are worthy of all the work it takes to keep you alive. Your body loves you. Your own body loves you.

If you are open to it, feel free to place your palms on your hips, take a deep, rejuvenating breath in, and allow the energy from your palms to flow into the bowl at the base of your torso. Now release that beautiful life breath, surrendering to this present moment.

You are safe, my friend.

Affirmation for Today:
I believe I am worthy of love.

And you are. Namaste.

The Second Day

Welcome to your second day. Find yourself in as comfortable a position as possible. You may want to invite specific attention to your hands and your feet. How are your feet situated? How are your hands feeling?

If you're called to, take a moment to spread your fingers wide, stretching them, and then furl them into a tight ball. Repeat this several times until you feel aliveness spreading all throughout your hand.

Do the same now with your toes. You may need to adjust your posture. Curl your toes, and then spread them out, stretching your feet. Do this a few times. Allow your breath to guide you. Inhale as you curl your toes, exhale as you spread them. The flow of your breathing will naturally dictate the rhythm of the movement.

(If you cannot move your hands or feet, you may begin to

SELF LOVED | 5

tighten and release another part of your body. Perhaps you could contract and release the muscles of your belly instead.)

Return to a comfortable, resting position, inviting stillness into the hands and feet. Take a moment here to notice the sensations in these areas. Is there any buzzing or vibration in your palms? Perhaps there are tingles or warmth in your toes? This is your life force energy. It is always here. Always ready to have the light of awareness cast upon it. Let's do our body the great honor of sitting in the presence of its experience. In the physical plane, we might find jewels of wisdom. Is there any sensation in your physical body that is calling out for more attention than others? Is your right shoulder kinked? Is your knee feeling achy? Is there pressure in your sinus? Sit with anything that arises. Do your best to be the detective of sensation. Find these feelings, and then sit with them. It takes great courage, determination, and focus, and I know you can do it.

Thoughts plucked from a time and place foreign to this present moment might pierce your awareness. This is as it should be. Do not fight the thoughts. Bringing your attention to the thinking mind is part of this practice. If you can begin to recognize that you are thinking, that you are being pulled from this moment, *that* is the practice. Notice. Invite awareness. Return to your body.

Then the next step is about free will. It's about choice.

We then get to choose what to do with the awareness of the thought. Do we indulge the thought? Or do we return to the present? For now, if you can, I would invite you to recognize your next inevitable thought. Can you watch the thought? If the thought were a physical entity, an object or a shape, where would it exist in your consciousness? In a moment, close your eyes. Then, as the light plays on the other side of your eyelids, allow yourself to be guided by the position of the thought. Can you find the thought? If it has vanished, you may simply return to the practice of scanning your physical body, inviting gentle awareness all throughout your being. From crown to toes, from outside in. You may now close your eyes.

∞

If you are able to place the thought, then you can direct it. You can choose to move it somewhere else.

Let's say you are driving, and an object appears on the road ahead of you. I grant you the power to move that object, to direct it out of your path. Begin to practice this. See if you can move it to either the right or the left of the road. Once you are able to do this, keep driving.

∞

If you are not a visual person, anytime you notice a thought, you can thank the thought. Our thoughts are trying to help us. They are usually trying to protect us from perceived danger. They want to keep us safe, but that also means they want to keep us small, afraid, and armored up. They don't want us to expand and venture onto a new, uncharted path. That would be too threatening for the ego mind. The ego mind wants to prevent harm or to warn us of harm it perceives to be imminent.

You could say to your thoughts, "Thank you for trying to help me," and then return your attention to the physical sensations in your body. Your entire meditation could likely consist of this cyclical pattern. Of noticing a single thought (or perhaps even noticing that you've been sucked down a rabbit hole of thought), thanking it, and returning to the physical feelings in your body. Noticing it, thanking it, and returning to the sensations you feel. Noticing it, thanking it, and coming home to your body. This in and of itself would be a beautiful practice. Be gentle with yourself.

Wherever you are, whatever you are moving through in this process, take some time to scan your body, inviting your awareness into this vast plane of sensations, and practice this technique.

Gently place your hands on the crown of your head, fingers together. Allow your hands to mold into the contours of your head. This is your crown chakra, seventh of the primary chakras, Sahasrara. Simply rest your hands here, and allow the energy from your palms to enter the sacred space. This is our connection to Source energy. To the energy of the Universe. Allow whatever sensations float into your consciousness to rest gently in your awareness.

You might begin to open your elbows outward on your inhale and bring them together on your exhale, keeping your hands on your crown. If any imagery arises, notice it. Thank it. Return to your breath.

You, my friend, are divine.

Affirmation for Today:
I am a being of divine light.

The Third Day

Welcome to our third day of practice. Find yourself in as comfortable a position as possible. Let's begin today by placing a hand on your low belly. Allow your breath to slow to its natural rhythm. Draw your attention to the space where your hand makes contact with your belly. You may even bid your other hand to come down as well, cradling this sacred space. Rest in the awareness of your experience here. Notice any feelings that arise. Heat from your palms, tingling, an opening sensation; anything and everything is available to be discovered in this vast plane of experience. Take a moment here.

Let's begin to explore a new dimension of sensation, a new field of energy. We have explored the physical plane, witnessing sensations in our body. Now we will venture into a deeper field. The emotional plane. Just as we scanned our physical bodies for sensations, I would now ask you to focus on any emotions that surface. Physical and emotional sensations are not separate. They are inextricably linked, making it difficult to discern the difference between them. If you are struggling with this distinction, simply set a clear intention. You might say to yourself or aloud, "What emotions are here? Can I uncover any emotions I wasn't aware of before beginning this practice? What am I feeling? What is here?" Sit with yourself in stillness, allowing these queries to float in your awareness while you place your hands on your low belly in this gesture of care and compassion.

∞

If you are not able to detect any emotions, or you are unsure whether these are emotions or physical sensations, I would urge you to continue treading the path. If something comes up, very likely there is a reason for it. Once we have set our intention, it is helpful to trust that when something arises, it is in service of that intention. Trust that if a feeling surfaces, it is here for you to examine. That feeling is offered to you for your growth. Perhaps it is a physical sensation tethered to an emotion, in which case I urge you to sit with that feeling. Bring your attention to the location of that feeling, perhaps even place a hand there if that's available. Sit with it and breathe. Sometimes all we need do is hold space for an emotion in order for it to reveal itself. You might even say, "It's ok. You're safe. You can reveal yourself to me. I am strong enough to remain present with you."

∞

If an emotion feels painful or overwhelming, I implore you to listen to what it might want, what it might need. To what you might want, to what you might need. Would it feel nice to take a deep breath? Would it feel supportive to shake your body? To rock back and forth? To cross your arms in front of your chest and rub your hands on your opposite arms? To cry? To push your palms together with increasing pressure? To make a sound? To sigh? To stretch? To say something out loud?

Start to attune to what your body wants when you are experiencing an emotion. This is a practice we can, and probably will, return to time and time again throughout our journey. Take a moment here to familiarize yourself with this method.

This is a challenging discipline, and I'm sending you love and support while you move through this. You may begin to ask yourself, "is there anything I am unwilling to feel?" See what response you receive when you ask this. Take some time.

You are so brave for venturing into this arena. We have created space for physical sensations, and we are now creating space for emotions. Is it possible for you to carve out space for gentleness here as well? You deserve to be tender with yourself. See if you are able to invite a nurturing energy into your investigation.

This gentle energy may guide you to places you didn't expect to travel. It may ask you to move on from emotions that become too painful. It may remind you that underneath all of your complex clusters of emotions, you are still whole. You remain intact. You are a strong, powerful, sensitive, open, emotional being who is brave enough to plumb the depths of your emotions. As you embark on this, at times, terrifying expedition, know that you are among a very small few who have the courage to look within. So many people numb themselves from the experience of their emotional lives. I made this mistake for much of my life. However, as we cultivate a practice of emotional awareness, we are not only building up a tolerance to suffering, we are also creating more space to experience the full expression of joy in our lives. This is the work. I am so proud of you for being here, for caring about yourself enough to show up.

∞

Take a deep breath. Let it float in and around your body, filling all the tender places we visited today. Allow yourself some time and space to process this experience. This is the process of self-regulation. Give yourself the gift of presence, of care and gentleness while you move through it.

Place your hands, once again, on your low belly. This is a beautiful gesture of wholeness. Reminding you that you are not broken. You are whole just as you are. You are healing.

You have the power to sit with your emotions. Namaste.

Affirmation for Today:
I balance my emotions in this sacred body of my soul.

The Fourth Day

Let us begin by finding a comfortable position, a gentle position. Take some time, really take time here, to listen to your body and hear what it wants or needs from you in order to feel comfortable. We've done this a few times now, and hopefully, we're beginning to form a foundation upon which to build our practice.

Start to listen to your body's messages about what it wants. What position would be most supportive for you today? It might be different from yesterday. It might be different from tomorrow. It might even differ from a few hours hence. But right here, right now, what does your body want? Take some time to be with yourself. Breathe deep, and listen.

Many practices teach us how exactly to sit or lie down or kneel in order to meditate. They highlight the best, most ideal positions for our practice. I've never been very fond of this idea. I suppose it's my inner rebel, but I believe this practice to be a wholly personal one, and for me, the beauty

SELF LOVED | 15

of our meditation practice is about connecting to ourselves. Listening to our inner rhythms and messages. Finding space for our own experience in a world that insists we fit into certain boxes and follow certain rules. I try to ignore "rules" when it comes to meditation. We have enough of that to contend with outside of this path. Here, I would encourage you to ignore anything, including the content of this book in fact, that is counter to your own innermost guidance. If you would like to practice meditation while dancing around your bedroom or going for a run. Please, do that. All I ask of you is to do it. To dedicate this time to yourself. Allow your inner life to unfold. Get curious about what's underneath all of the "supposed-tos" and above all, be kind and patient with yourself.

Once you have arrived in as comfortable a position as possible, allow your breath to move to the forefront of your attention. Follow your breath in, down, through...up, and out. In, down, through...up, and out. If we can follow our breath, there may be great lessons waiting to be learned. Our breath is our instructor. We must open and receive the wisdom of this loving teacher. Follow, accept, let it flow.

We aren't affecting our breath; we are following. It might change as we follow it, in the same way our performance might be influenced by the presence of an observer. In becoming aware of the attention paid to it, our breath might start to shift, to flow differently. Slower, faster, deeper, more shallow. Whatever occurs, just follow and open. Open yourself to any lessons your breath whispers to you as you arrive here and now with your body and your breath.

If judgment or fear arise, acknowledge them, thank them for their concern, move them to the side of the road, and keep on going.

Now if you are open to it, imagine a glimmering light coming down from the sky. It floats down toward you, and on your next inhale, it enters your third eye through your brow. It is cool and refreshing. On your exhale, it pours out of your nose or mouth. On each inhale, this cool, glimmering light penetrates your brow and fills up your whole body, flowing all throughout. Then on your exhale, it moves outward back to its source. There is an assembly here. The cool light flows in, around, and through, then leaves. In, down, through…up, and out. In, down, through…up, and out. Filling you with light. Filling you with glimmering light.

With each breath, there is more space created by this flowing light. If this light encounters any darkness, any sticky, dull places in you, it has the power to blast through them. A power washer of sorts, breaking down the debris in your body and flushing it out on your exhale. With each breath you grow cleaner, clearer. With each inhale, you cleanse your mind; with each exhale, you cleanse your body. Scrubbing

SELF LOVED | 17

the inside of your frame until you are a vessel of pure light. Glimmering from the inside out. Cool, refreshed, cleansed.

You may notice a slight buzzing in your brow, a vibration. Bring your attention here, and see what you find. Is there any tension in this space? Can you detect other sensations? Is there perhaps a message waiting here? An image? A voice? What is here? Maybe nothing. Maybe everything. Take a moment to invite some tenderness into this space. Perhaps even saying to yourself or aloud, "I am here to listen if you want to share your secrets. I trust in your wisdom. I trust in your vision. I gladly bear witness to whatever you would like to share. I listen with loving ears. I watch with loving eyes."

As you observe, you may want to place the pad of a finger on your brow. When I say brow, it's really the center of your forehead, the area between your eyebrows and hairline. Right in the middle. The area is quite simple, but sometimes not so easy, to feel. It is simply the place that feels the most alive when you touch it. For me, the best way to describe it is the place that feels right. Gently touch your face around this area and see if there is a spot that, to put it plainly, just hits different. It is a subtle sensation, so if it is not immediately available to you, be patient. It might take a moment, so for now, place your entire palm on your forehead with the pinky finger along the brow line. As we bring physical touch to this area, perhaps we can start to imagine the glimmering light entering in through our palm, moving through our bodies, and leaving through our third eye. Creating a beautiful cycle of light. Breathe in through this space and out through this space. This kind of attention invites an activation into this chakra. As we attend to this area, we open this wheel of energy, inviting it to spin faster and faster. Vibrating, buzzing with aliveness.

Stay with the sensation and with the space that is created here. Any visions that present themselves, greet them with openness. If you don't understand the message, just thank it, and continue to observe. Continue to bear witness to the power of your intuitive mind. If judgment arises, thank the judgment, and guide it to the side of the road. Stay with the path. You are mastering your mind. It is a subtle, gentle, and powerful practice that takes great focus and courage to engage in. Stay with it, bear witness, feel the feelings, trust the message. If nothing arises, that is a message as well. If you are thinking and doubting, this is an opportunity to open further, listen more deeply, trust more fully. Or to simply reconnect with your body. To feel into this space and see what is present.

Take a final breath of cool, glimmering light, and on your exhale, allow a sound to release from your mouth.

Thank you for joining me for this meditation. We are beginning to arrive. Here and now. Your mind thanks you for cleansing it. You might even thank your inner eye. "Thank you for these lessons. I will allow them to float in my awareness without attachment to an understanding. I greet the gifts of your wisdom with love."

You are connected, my friend.

Affirmation for Today:
Intuition speaks to me freely, and I listen with a loving mind.

The Fifth Day

Welcome to your fifth day of practice. What an incredible gift you are bestowing upon yourself, to arrive in presence, to give of yourself, to lean into the unknown in hopes of accessing something new. This is true vulnerability. To trust enough in your strength that you can leap and then look. In a gesture of love, place your hands on your opposite shoulders and bow your head, or if that's not comfortable for you, bring your palms together outside your heart center. Take a moment to connect with yourself here. You are beginning to unravel the woven narratives that no longer serve you. You are starting to tread the path of awakening. It is an endless road and one we must walk daily. Let's begin.

No matter where you are, move your hands toward your solar plexus, just a few inches above your belly button. Take a moment to connect with this sacred space. What is here? As you place your hand on this tender area, do any feelings arise? Bear witness to these.

SELF LOVED | 21

Start to bring your attention to your breath as well. Do your hands rise and fall with your breath? Is there any movement here?

You might experience tummy grumbles. This is a great indication of inner flow. From an energetic perspective, movement indicates health, and stagnancy indicates a lack of health. As part of this work, we are trying to create space for more fluidity in every aspect of our lives. More physical movement, more energetic movement. This is all part of the process of healing.

Let's take one more deep breath, and on your exhale, release a sound. Any sound.

With your hands on your upper belly, I would like to ask you a few questions. Just allow them to wash over you. If an answer comes, observe it. If not, just remain here, present with your own aliveness, with the life flowing through your body. If any of these questions trigger shame or discomfort, do not run away. Sit with the feelings. Perhaps you might ask further questions about what is underneath the discomfort. Is this something you have yet to process? Are you clenching onto a belief that no longer serves you? Investigate what's here, and beyond all of this, be kind to yourself. Remember, you deserve your own compassion.

When do you feel the most confident?

∞

What do you do that makes you smile?

∞

What do you admire about yourself?

∞

When are you the most productive?

∞

What is something you did this week that made you feel strong?

∞

Return home. Check in and see what's going on in your physical body. Is there any tightness or tension? Does your body feel differently from when you began this practice today? Take a moment with yourself, and invite curiosity about what you witness.

∞

I would like you to imagine for me a version of yourself in the future. This version of you spends most days feeling how you feel at your most confident. They seem very purposeful and powerful, and yet they often do things that make you smile. You can't help but admire them. They are deliberate and have great mastery over their productivity. They understand the way they work, and they honor it. They try not to compare themselves to other people. They practice sitting with their feelings and building up a tolerance to uncomfortable emotions. This has made them more comfortable, easy to be around. Easy to be. They are grounded and yet free, joyful. It is beautiful to behold.

Please take a deep, rejuvenating breath, and let's return to this present moment. How was it to hold space for this version of yourself? Did you feel excited to think of yourself in this way?

The moment you decide that you want something, it has begun to move toward you. It is now about trusting the process and moving forward with the knowledge that what is meant for you is on its way.

As you move through your day today, you might ask yourself, "What would that version of me do in this situation?" Begin to familiarize your conscious mind with who you want to be. Doing so will enable you to bring this more aligned version of yourself into reality. Welcoming your future self into the present.

You are powerful beyond measure. Namaste.

Affirmation for Today:
Anything is possible. I am ready for my new life.

The Sixth Day

Let's take a few deep breaths here as we arrive in our desired position for practice today. You may want to begin experimenting with different hand positions. You could place one hand on your heart and the other on your belly or bring your palms together with the thumbs touching the forehead. You could also simply clasp the opposite elbow in a gesture of safety and love. Play around here and see what feels good for you today.

Once you are comfortable and you've arrived in the here and now, this beautiful present moment, gently guide your awareness to your throat. What is here? When your attention drifts into this space, what do you find? Does anything come up? Do you notice tension? Do you notice any thoughts surfacing? Any to-do lists, or plans starting to arise? Take stock of what is here. If you begin to judge yourself, thank the judgmental voice and calmly direct it to the side of the road—the corner of your consciousness. Everyone is allowed on your path, even judgment, but you still get to decide who is in the forefront of your vision. Trust in the power and strength of your mind.

∞

Did anything arrive once you brought your awareness here? Perhaps, all of a sudden you were flooded by unwanted thoughts, or a tightness arose that wasn't there before you brought attention here. These are all important messages, and you can recognize these in the landscape of your journey while you continue to tread the path ahead. You are here, and so is this tension. You are present, and so are these thoughts. Hold space for what is here, whatever that might be, and be kind to yourself. Knowing that you are not alone and that whatever comes up has nothing to do with your inherent value. Observe, and invite curiosity into this space.

∞

If you are comfortable with it, gently place your hands on your neck. You can put them on the back of the neck, on the front, on the sides, or you can hover your hands in front of your throat. Whatever gesture you choose, do it with the intention of guiding more energy into this space. Our mental energy is here, and with this gesture we bring physical attention here as well. This can be a sensitive area, so obviously, we want to be very gentle with this tender space. Take a few breaths here, and with each inhale, say to yourself, "I trust the power of my voice" with each exhale, say, "I love my voice."

∞

When we invite awareness into this area, we may start to notice times in our lives when our throat closes, when it feels tight, almost as if something is stuck there. This is your truth. When you notice that tension, it might be there to nudge you in a different direction. There could be something you aren't communicating, and because your throat chakra trusts you and believes in the value of your truth, it wants you to express yourself honestly. That's why it's there, to guide you toward ultimate self-expression. If we can connect with our truth, if we can believe in the power of our story, of our unique voice, and share it with love and compassion, then our throat chakras will smile upon us with light.

∞

Often, we feel tightness in the throat when experiencing a particularly challenging emotion, an emotion we don't want to feel. Shame, self-doubt, nervousness, or fear can all trigger a blockage in this chakra.

If at any point today or in the future, you notice this tightness arise, I would offer you the following guidance:

If you are experiencing a challenging emotion and you notice your throat start to close, you may want to place a hand gently on this area (I prefer to rest my hand on the back of my neck, but whatever feels best for you) and the other on your low belly. You might say, "I am strong enough to feel this feeling. I honor my body's need to feel this right now."

If you are experiencing shame or self-doubt, I invite you to place a hand on your throat and the other on your upper belly, just a few fingers above your navel. You may say, "I don't have to believe everything I think. I have great value, just as I am."

If you are experiencing fear or anxiety when you notice your throat close up, you could place one hand just below the crease where your hip hinges and the other on your throat and say, "I am here, I am safe, the earth is supporting me, I trust myself."

I encourage you to revisit this section the next time you experience a painful or challenging emotion. (Feel free to dog-ear this page).

∞

Now, return to this present moment. Take a few more deep breaths, and with each inhale, imagine a cool blue light entering in and filling up your throat, and on your exhale, imagine the light gleaming brighter and brighter.

∞

With each inhale, your throat expands, it grows larger. On your exhale, it grows stronger, more open. Inhale and expand, exhale and strengthen. Continue this for a few more breaths.

∞

If you are still experiencing tension here, I'd like you to assign that tension a physical shape. Imagine it is an ice cube. The size of the ice cube depends on the level of pressure. Take a moment to feel the ice cube of tension in your throat.

∞

On your next inhale, I want you to breathe in through your mouth. As the oxygen flows in your mouth and down your throat, the warmth of your breath begins to slowly melt the ice cube. With each breath, the ice cube melts a little more, and you can feel it getting smaller and smaller. You may even swallow and feel the ice cube turn to water and move onward, down your throat. Then, on your last swallow, notice that it is gone.

∞

Return your hands to the comfortable position you established at the beginning of our session today. How are you feeling? What is here? Has anything changed? Do you feel any different from when you started this session?

∞

Thank you for joining me today. Take a few deep, rejuvenating breaths to seal this practice.

You are open and expressive. Namaste.

Affirmation for Today:
I believe in the power of my story, and I am brave enough to share it.

The Seventh Day

Congratulations on making it through the first week of your practice! Compound knowledge is building, and you are sowing the seeds now that will reap an abundant harvest in the future. Just keep going, my friend. I'm so proud of you.

For this session, we will be focusing on your heart space. There are seven days in a week and seven primary chakras. The heart is the center of these chakras.

We will be doing some movement in this one, so make sure you're situated in a way that you can easily place your hands on different parts of your body throughout this practice. Let's begin.

Take a few deep, rejuvenating breaths and arrive right here, right now.

∞

If you're open to it, place your hands on your heart space. On your next comfortable inhale, I invite you to say, "I receive love," and on your exhale, "I give love." Repeat this mantra, guided by your breath, for several cycles.

∞

What would it mean to move from a place of love? To choose love? In every aspect of your life, how can you choose love more often? I want to open some space for you to ruminate on this for a moment.

∞

When we speak about moving from love, I don't mean denying your emotions, smiling when you feel like crying, betraying your boundaries, or appeasing someone who is being rude or unkind. What I am referring to is rather the act of looking deeply at your emotions and, before leaping to a conclusion about what they might mean about you, try sitting with them instead. Can you choose to love yourself through these intense emotions? When you feel like crying, can you decide to love yourself while you cry and maybe to love yourself while you feel embarrassed about crying? When someone challenges a boundary, can you choose to love yourself enough to reaffirm those boundaries, recognizing that you are worthy of your own comfort, care and safety? Can you choose to love enough to stick up for yourself and others when someone is being unkind? On the outside, it may look the same whether love exists or not. We might hold our boundaries firmly whether we are moving from love or from some other place. However, when we move from love, when we choose love, we lighten our load, and we begin to vibrate on a different level. You feel different. Take a moment to think of ways that you can choose love.

∞

I believe we are all capable of giving and receiving love. One of the most powerful aspects of love is presence. *Here* and *now* are the backbones of love, and in this practice of meditation, you are beginning to unlock the possibility of opening your heart to the flow of love. In and out. Giving and receiving.

Take a moment to see if you can invite any love into your breath. How can you breathe from love? How can you inhale love? How can you exhale love?

∞

Love is here whether we choose to notice it or not. It will be here always, a constant. We might try to bury it underneath piles and piles of doubt and judgment, but it will always be here. What we are engaging in while we practice together is removing the debris we've packed around our hearts so that we can more deeply feel into our experience and love ourselves while we do it. You are the only one who knows your journey, and you are the only one who can love yourself as you walk the path. How can you love yourself more fully? How can you love others more fully? Take some time here to feel your hands on your heart space, sending love to yourself, and remember that you have love underneath everything else you encounter. There is love at the core of your being. It sits underneath the foundation of all of your thoughts. There is love. How can you dive deeper and begin to find it?

∞

Wiggle your toes now, and perhaps even place your hands on your feet if that's available to you. Feel the love they give you every day. They choose to carry you. They prevent you from tripping (most of the time), they keep you upright and able to move about. They love you enough to trust the direction you choose for them. They love you.

Maybe you can show them some love. Perhaps you could slide your fingers in the spaces between your toes and slowly and gently push through, and pull upward. And as you do this, you can say, "I am so grateful for you, for all that you do. I send love to you."

∞

Perhaps you move your hands up to your shins and calves. Feel your physical body, and as you send love to this space, say, "I am here."

∞

Now move up to your knees. See if you can give love to your knees, saying, "I am so grateful for this body."

∞

Place your hands on your thighs and hamstrings. Feeling the strength and love your legs have as they carry you around. You might say, "Thank you." Really take time to be with yourself here.

∞

Move your hands up to your hips. See what it would feel like to send love into this space. You may say, "I am safe."

∞

Now place your hand on your low belly a few inches below your navel. "I am creative and emotionally available."

∞

Move your hands up just a few fingers above your navel. "I am strong and resilient."

∞

Place your hands on your heart space, "I am loved." Can you feel any expansion here?

∞

Move your hands gently up to your neck. See if you can send love to this space. "I am expressive."

∞

Place your palms on your forehead. "I am connected to my intuition."

∞

Now place both hands on the crown of your head, "I am divine."

∞

Shake your hands out and place them palm to palm outside of your heart center, prayer hands.

You can choose to move from a place of love. This is something you can choose. You can choose today, tomorrow, and the next day. You can't choose yesterday, and that's ok. We have to let that go. Today we can choose to love our yesterday selves and release what we can no longer control about what we've done. All of us must do that. We all have things we would do differently if we had them to do again. If we didn't, then we wouldn't be growing. Fortunately for all of us, we can dedicate ourselves to growth and expansion. The best path is to choose love, send love to our past selves, and release what we can no longer control.

∞

It is the purest form of human expression, to love. Love asks nothing of the giver or receiver. Love exists to be expressed. To be felt. To be shared. When we start to ask ourselves, "how can we move from love?" we are really asking, "how can we connect more deeply with the light that we know exists in all of us?" You have that light. And through this practice, we are slowly learning how to unearth it. Remove all the dirt around this space so that you can shine the brighter. And you will. We will. Together.

∞

Love flows easily to and from your heart. You are loving. You are loved.

Affirmation for Today:
__I am overflowing with eternal love, and I share this love easily with those around me.__

The Eighth Day

For today's meditation, we will be doing something slightly different. We are going to journey into a new realm, the astral realm.

As usual, I would like you to find as comfortable a position as possible, and begin to take a few deep, rejuvenating breaths, arriving here and now.

∞

If any thoughts arise, thank them, and keep on trucking down the road. Just breathe.

∞

Now, I would like for you to become very aware of your body. What sensations are you feeling? From toes to crown, can you pinpoint the feelings in your body? I encourage you to really tap into your physical field here. What do you feel? Any tension? Any tightness? Try to connect with what's going on in your body. Be an observer, watch for new sensations, try to detect anything that arises. Just explore here for a moment.

∞

If you're able, I would like for you to extend this search. Can you tap into the more subtle sensations? Perhaps you feel a buzzing? A tingling? Heat? Cool? Or something else. Something more. If nothing comes up, that's ok. Just keep searching. Keep seeking.

∞

Taking the time to search, that's what matters. It is in the practice that we grow, not in what we find but rather in what we seek. It's through the consistency of our practice that we start to bloom.

I'm going to ask you to close your eyes in a moment, and imagine that all of your sensations, those physical and energetic, are creating a field that you can begin to see. You can picture your entire body from crown to toes. Close your eyes and start to look for this field of energy.

∞

Begin to merge your conscious mind with this energy field. Allow your conscious mind, the one here that is reading these words, allow this conscious mind to meld with your energy field. Whatever this means to you, just give it a try. If you simply hold these two ideas in your mind, that's ok. If you are simply breathing and wondering what I mean, that's ok too. Just sit with this.

∞

The energy field now takes on the contours, size, and shape of your physical body, and it begins to rise a few inches above you. If you are lying down, it is hovering right above your body. If you are seated, it floats out in front of you.

∞

You are the energy field. Notice that you can move as this energy field. Explore here. See if you can float upward. Try gliding around the room or space you're in. See what you're capable of as this energy body. We can call this astral play. See if you can invite a lighthearted curiosity to what you do here.

∞

Explore this space from different angles. See how high you can get, how low to the ground. Start to notice this space and observe it with the inquisitiveness of a child.

∞

Now that you have explored some of what you're capable of as this energy body, turn and gaze upon your physical self. Your physical body still resides in the same location, resting in the same posture. Take a moment to look at your physical body. Your hair, arms, legs, face. What do you see here? What are you looking at? Do you notice anything? What do you see when you look at yourself from this perspective? Take some time here.

∞

If you are not able to connect with this notion of transcending the physical form, that's ok too. Simply trying to invite the energy of playfulness here can be a powerful process. Just observe. See what comes up. If you are judging yourself, notice it, acknowledge the judging thought, and send it to the side of the road. Continue to explore.

∞

Take a few breaths to return to your body, allowing the astral and the physical realms to merge. With each breath, they become more solidly connected until they are one.

When we can float out of our physical experience for a moment, we can begin to attune to our energetic field. If we practice this transcendence, we can start to really recognize the subtle energies that exist within and around us with greater ease.

You are a being of light, floating in the great sea of consciousness. Namaste.

Affirmation for Today:
I am ceaselessly curious about the life within me. I invite curiosity into the unknown. I take joy in discovering the uncharted territory of my soul.

The Ninth Day

Welcome to your ninth day of practice. Nine is a number associated with completion, with the closing of cycles. Hopefully, this helps you close and release anything in your life that is no longer serving you. We do this in order to open ourselves to those aspects which bring us love and joy.

Start in a comfortable position, and let's begin to breathe into this moment. Take some time to connect with your body. Invite some awareness, and ask what is present.

∞

I'd like for you to call to mind someone who is very dear to you. Someone you love. If no one is immediately available to you, you can call to mind someone who has passed or even a beloved pet. Hold them in your mind. See if you can imagine this person fully. In all of their wonder and uniqueness.

∞

If there was a color you would associate with them, what

would it be? Allow this color to fill their body and the space around it.

∞

Notice that they are smiling. Greet their smile with a slight, gentle smile as well. Take some time to be present with them.

∞

Imagine that as you two bask in the presence of one another, a light begins to shine from a space in the center of your forehead. Your third eye. It is tingly and warm, and very slowly, it begins to flow out of your brow, through the air, over to them. It starts to float into their forehead, creating a brilliant light in their third eye. There is an endless flow of this light pouring from you, and it continues to enter them. You are both smiling slightly, connecting through time and space. Be together here.

∞

You may reach out a hand to hold theirs. When they take your hand, a light ignites at the point of contact and begins to glow brighter and brighter. Perhaps you take their other hand and bow your heads to meet, forehead to forehead, third eyes kissing. The light that flows out of your brow is now at its brightest, emanating brilliantly in a great orb of purest white. Breathe into this light. Allow it to fill you up. Watch as it fills them as well. Breathe and open. Soften and flow.

∞

Slowly release their hands. You are both shining brightly all throughout your bodies. Even the air around you is glimmering with light. Neither has dimmed since releasing contact. Rather, you are glowing all the brighter for having sat in the presence of this union. Send gratitude to them for sharing in this beautiful connection.

∞

Take a few breaths to return to this present moment. You might place a hand on your brow. This light is inside of you. You are filled with glimmering light.

∞

You are connected, through time, through space, to all living beings and each other. Namaste.

Affirmation for Today:
My gratitude for my loved ones fills me with light and strength.

The Tenth Day

Welcome to today's practice.

It is enormously important that we express ourselves. When we hide away our truth in order to appease others or avoid conflict, vulnerability, or judgment, we are taking away the remarkable experience of connecting with our true selves. We are also robbing others of a chance to get to know who we really are. Today, let's try to connect with the importance of self-expression.

Take a few slow, rejuvenating breaths to settle into today's practice. You are here on this path for a reason. Honor yourself for committing this time to your practice, to yourself.

∞

On your next comfortable breath, I would like for you to release a sound on your exhale. Allow it to fill the entire length of your exhale. It can be any sound. Just release a sound with your breath.

∞

Now, I would like for you to do the same, but release another sound, different from before.

∞

This time, I would like for you to release a funny sound.

∞

I would like you now to release a word. Any word.

∞

And now, another word.

∞

Another word.

∞

Another.

∞

Another.

∞

If you're open to it, place your hands on either side of your neck. Imagine your neck getting stronger and stronger. Imagine your throat filling with light and expanding within your neck. The muscles are protecting this sacred place and giving it room to grow and shine, radiating the beautiful light of your truth.

∞

What color is this light? Can you imagine a color in your throat? It's cooling, refreshing. What is this color?

∞

Allow your hands to hold the light of this space. Your throat is now glimmering. It is large and powerful. Take a moment here to focus on something you'd like to say. It doesn't matter to whom or what it is. I just want you to hold space for this communication. It doesn't have to make sense. What comes up when I ask you what you'd like to say right now? If you could say anything to anyone right now, what would that be? Sit with that, and start to frame the words that you might say.

∞

When you're ready, take a deep breath in, and say those words on your next exhale. You can yell them, whisper them, or sing them, but I would like for you to say them aloud.

∞

I would like for you to repeat this process. Allow some time to let the next message come to you. Let it form in your mind and your heart. What would you most like to say at this moment? Right here, right now, what do you most want to express? Take some time to ruminate and allow the words to form.

∞

Now, take another deep, supportive breath, and let these words out.

∞

For many of us, expression can be one of the most challenging hurdles to overcome. We are told that our voice isn't valuable, that our words are weak, that our truth is inaccurate. We might have been told that we are not saying the right thing, that we aren't good at communicating, that we are too loud, too quiet, too anything. But that's even more of a reason for us to connect with our self-expression.

Remember, your throat chakra wants you to express yourself. It will support you if you do. So, trust that you are being supported by energies all around you that you can't see, and begin to practice expressing yourself. If you find this particularly difficult, then I would suggest adding this practice into your daily routine. Take a few moments each day to breathe deeply, then say something you want to say on your exhale. Do this for three rounds each day. Breathing normally for several cycles in between each one. If you start to employ this practice on a regular basis, I think you'll be amazed at how much more aligned your throat chakra becomes. It will beam with gratitude.

∞

You express yourself with confidence and strength.

Affirmation for Today:
I am expressive. I communicate with honesty and ease.

The Eleventh Day

Welcome to our practice today. Let's begin in a seated position if that's comfortable for you. Breathe deeply and fully. With each exhale, let go of any physical tension that is available to release. Your shoulders, your brow, your jaw. Release tension in your chest, your belly, your hips, your legs.

∞

Now tap into a more subtle release. See if you can cast away any tension in the eye area. How about the top of your head? Is there any tension here you can release? What about your palms? Your heels? Try to let go of the more acute blockages you encounter. Perhaps you could release the insides of your muscles? How would it feel to release tension in the middle of your head? In your organs? Just as a practice, see what happens when you bring awareness to different areas inside your physical body with the intention of releasing. See what comes up. It may be nothing. It may be something marvelous. Breathe and release. Explore here.

∞

Do you notice any emotions rising to the surface? Is there any space in your body that is holding emotional tension? Perhaps the areas you've been releasing are already connected to emotions. If that's the case, continue the work of releasing these physical and emotional blockages. If you have only been noticing physical tension, now bring some awareness to the emotional plane. Is there any part of you that feels emotionally raw or uncomfortable? Be here with this. Release any tension you encounter if you can. If not, continue to scan your body, open to discovery.

∞

Bring your palms together in prayer position at your heart center. This is also called gassho. Take a moment here to connect with your heart space. Is there any tension in this space? If so, take some time with it. We won't be releasing that tension right away. Instead, I would like for you to investigate it. See if you can hold that tension in your awareness. Try not to change it. Just observe. If you notice other tension in your body, which is natural, gently encourage a release of that other tension while you focus on your heart center. It's a subtle but challenging exercise.

Take long, cooling breaths, and be patient with yourself.

∞

If you don't experience any tension in your heart space, continue to breathe and release tension in your body. If you do notice tension in the heart space, imagine it's a tuft of cotton candy, fibrous and delicate. Begin to pull at the tension.

As you peel it away, a section of this tension is freed. Once separated, it begins to dissolve like candy floss in the rain.

∞

After doing this for some time, there is only a small tuft of tension remaining. I would like you to examine this tension now. Is it a physical or emotional tension? What is the most uncomfortable or painful part of this tension? Take time to look at this small remaining piece, and see if you can examine it with eyes of love. Can you pull it apart any further?

Once it is as small as you can make it, hold onto this tiny piece of tension, and ask what is at the core of this discomfort. Be gentle with yourself. Self-compassion is the strongest path here. Invite kindness as you parse through this discomfort. There are energies all around you supporting you in this journey. As am I.

∞

When you're ready, you may release this tension. Offer it up to the rain. Watch it dissolve. Watch it dissipate until it completely disappears.

Then return to your breath. Breathe long, slow, cooling breaths. Let the breath fill your entire body, and then release it. Letting go of any residual tension.

∞

With your palms together at your heart center, bow your head to yourself. Acknowledging the strength in your loving practice. You may not believe it, but love is the most powerful practice we can engage in. Love for others, and love for ourselves. You grow stronger every time you choose love.

∞

You are filled with eternal love. You are loved eternally. Namaste.

Affirmation for Today:
I am a beacon of hope for the unexamined parts of my soul. I guide them to the light of love so that they may be fully felt and heard and, finally, laid to rest.

The Twelfth Day

Welcome to your twelfth day of practice. I'm very proud of you. Do you feel proud of yourself for committing to this practice? Sticking with it this long is no small feat. It is incredibly challenging to dedicate yourself to your own development, and you have stuck with it for twelve days now. See if you can invite a sense of gratification into your physical body. Can you sense a joyful grin spreading itself across your belly just a few fingers above your belly button? Take some time to imagine this space is beaming; proud of you for having taken this time to care for yourself. Can you feel proud of yourself?

∞

Place your hand just above your belly button. This is your solar plexus. Begin to gently tap on this space. Imagine that as you tap, you are activating this chakra, inviting more confidence into your energy field.

∞

You might begin to rub this space, rub your hand on this area, and see if an aliveness begins to awaken here.

∞

Take a moment's pause. How is this space feeling? Does it feel tingly? Tight? Open? Free? What sensations arise when you bring your attention here? Are you more aware of it than when we began? Take some time and invite awareness to this space.

∞

Begin now to imagine that as you inhale, a sunny, yellow light enters in through this space, and as you exhale, it glows brighter. Continue to breathe. Warm light enters as you inhale and glows brighter on your exhale.

∞

The light now begins to fill your entire body. It floats up from your belly all the way to your crown, and down your legs all the way to your toes. As this vibrant, cheerful yellow light fills your vision, can you imagine your sense of self-worth growing? The light glows brighter and brighter while your worth grows stronger and stronger.

∞

This is always here. There is never a time when you are not being supported by your sense of self-worth, by your strength, by your resilient, confident self. This is always here. Let's take some time to acknowledge and appreciate this light.

∞

See if you can breathe into this space. If it's available to you, actually allow your upper belly to expand and move. You may place your hand here and watch it rise and fall with your breath. With each inhale, say to yourself or aloud, "I am strong and confident," and with each exhale, say, "I am resilient and powerful." Inhale and exhale. Feel more fully into these words with each breath.

∞

Place your palms together in prayer, and place your wrists on your solar plexus with your fingers pointing away from you. Continue to breathe into this space and see if you can make your hands move outward from your body on your inhale. You may want to begin opening your hands as you inhale, like a blossoming flower and closing when you exhale.

Your wrists might naturally inch away from your body as you practice this. Experiment.

∞

Try to exaggerate this gesture. You may even turn your gaze upward on your inhale as you splay open your hands. Try to invite some energy into your fingers. Open them as wide as you can on your inhale, and then furl them into little balls when you exhale, bowing your head. Allow your breath to guide your movements. In and out. Open and closed.

∞

Let's take one more deep breath in this way and then return to the natural flow of your breath. You are filled with sunny, vibrant light. Thank you for joining me today.

∞

You have great value, exactly as you are. Namaste.

Affirmation for Today:
I get to decide my worthiness. No one else determines my worth but me.

The Thirteenth Day

There is a sacred light inside of you. This light knows you better than you know yourself. It is all-seeing, all-knowing. Trust in this light. Allow this light to guide you.

Welcome to your meditation today. Take a slow, rejuvenating inhale, and feel the life-force breath filling your lungs. Now exhale, releasing any tension in your body. Inhale and allow the breath to enter and swirl all throughout your body, and exhale, clearing these channels, opening up your energy, and creating space for something new.

∞

Allow your breath to begin filling your low belly. On your exhale, release any tension in this space. Inhale and fill up your belly, exhale, and sink more deeply into this present moment.

∞

You are caring for your body, caring for your mind. This is such a gift. Thank yourself for the compassion you are bestowing upon yourself. Place your hands on your low belly, if you are open to it, and allow this loving energy to fill your sacral.

∞

I would like for you to extend your awareness to the world around you. What is the first thing you can hear?

(If this is not available to you, notice the vibrations around you instead.)

∞

Now the second thing? And the third?

∞

See if you can really feel into the presence of these sounds. Allow them to fill the entirety of your awareness. Notice any new sounds that arise. Begin the practice of recognizing what is around you by detecting each new sound that floats into your ears. Greet the new sound with attention, holding space to discover the newness of each one. These sounds may have already existed, but by bringing your awareness to them, they now arrive on your path. How much of our life is hidden from us, or rather, how many of us hide from the life around us? All we need do to live more fully is simply open our eyes to see what is already there. Open our minds, to hear what is underneath the noise.

∞

What is the farthest thing you can hear?

∞

Now the quietest? What is the softest sound?

∞

Lean into all of the noises. All of them at once. Inviting an awareness of the symphony, however faint, that has greeted your ears today. Welcome these sounds and revel in the beauty of your hearing. Grateful for your ability to listen to the vast aliveness of the world around you.

∞

Take time now to ground. Imagine a light shining from the center of your belly. You are filled with this divine light. Imagine it growing brighter with each inhale, and on each exhale, I want you to breathe out anything that is not this light.

∞

Bring your attention to the room around you. If you are not in a room, if you're outside, for example, then focus on the area surrounding you. Now, try to find three things around you that are green. If you are unable to find three, then find as many as you are able, and then focus on the color green. Focus on the green and see what happens when you fill your entire attention with this color.

∞

Now bring your attention to something white. Can you find something white? See how many white things you can find where you are.

∞

How about blue? Can you find something blue?

∞

Now black?

∞

Yellow?

∞

Purple?

∞

Take time to look about your space with "soft eyes." Eyes which see all. Try to extend the realm of your periphery. How far can you see in the space around you without moving your eyes? It is a practice, so be patient with yourself. You may need to focus on something in your direct line of sight, something not too distracting, something stationary. Be with it. Take your time.

∞

Gently guide your awareness to your body. Starting at your toes and moving upward, begin to invite awareness to each part of your body. Toes, feet, ankles, shins, calves, knees, and so on. Trace your entire physical body all the way up to your crown. Paying close attention to any sensations as you greet each body part with your attention. Do this with love. Any other emotions or thoughts you may be inflicting upon your experience, simply thank them and ask them to move to the side of your awareness. You will attend to these thoughts later if they need tending to.

∞

What did you find? Is anything here? Do you feel any areas of tightness or tension? If so, is there any way you can breathe into these areas and free up some space?

Take time to revisit any areas you encountered that you feel need your attention. Feel free to stretch, yawn, speak, cry, shake, or hum. Gently ask what this tension is requesting of you, and try your best to honor that request.

∞

With tenderness, invite your awareness back to your breath. Allow it to fill up your low belly. Notice the bright light, still gleaming within. Always there, always glowing, always filling you with light.

∞

You are an ocean of sensation. Lovingly aware of each crest and trough. Namaste.

Affirmation for Today:
I revel in the beauty of awareness.
I honor my own experience.

The Fourteenth Day

Congratulations on making it through the second week of your practice!

Today is going to be all about grounding. Grounding our energy, grounding our thoughts, grounding our bodies.

Let's begin by taking a few slow, deep breaths. Really try to track your breath as it flows in and as it flows out. Take a few moments to ground here in this present moment. Find as comfortable a position as possible, and gently guide your awareness to the part of your body that is making contact with the floor, the chair beneath you, your bed, whatever part of you that is being held. If you are seated in a chair, bring your attention to the spaces where your bottom meets the chair and where your feet meet the floor. If you are sitting on the floor, connect with every part of your body that is in contact with it. Take some time to really attend to the space where your body meets the support beneath it. Imagine this space is filled with light. The longer you bring your attention here, the brighter the light glows. Take some time and be here with yourself.

∞

Imagine that this place of contact with your support begins to grow roots that spread down into the earth. They spread through material objects, and they can penetrate the surface of the earth and push down through the earth's core. Connecting you with the entire world. Holding you, helping you to feel more stable, more secure. Take time to visualize these roots spreading down, down, down.

∞

You begin to notice that your roots are not the only ones down there. In fact, there is a vast network of roots, all weaving their way through this subterranean tapestry. You are connected to each other. Every single person has roots that hold them, support them, guide them. Roots that are in constant communication with us, that channel our thoughts and actions. They are some of our most dependable guides

∞

Once you become aware of the roots, they begin to glow. It starts from the point of contact, and it begins to flow down into the earth, lighting up the darkness below.

Other roots begin to glow, and the light slowly drizzles down into the core of the earth. As each new being becomes aware of their roots, their light glows brighter, spreading deeper and deeper into the earth.

∞

We are all connected. All of us. And the earth is here for us, to support us, to hold us. If you can invite awareness to what is here, you may begin to fully feel the healing love that is available to you all the time. The support that constantly surrounds you.

∞

You are grounded in love and light. Namaste.

Affirmation for Today:
My roots go deep and connect me with every living being. I am held and supported by the earth.

The Fifteenth Day

Today we are going to do a manifestation meditation. If you are new to this, be gentle with yourself and observe any sensations, emotions, or thoughts that arise. Greet them with compassion and witness any developments over the course of the next few weeks and months.

Begin by opening your hands and placing them in your lap, palms facing up. If you are lying down, you may place your hands on the ground beside you. Envision this as a posture of openness, receptivity. You are open and ready to receive. Take some time to find this and begin breathing slowly and deeply once you have arrived.

∞

I would like you to bring to mind something for which you are enormously grateful. I want this to be something you can truly connect with. Something that allows you to feel this gratitude all throughout your body. It could be a loved one, clean water, or your ability to walk. Whatever it is, make sure it's strong for you. Powerful.

∞

Begin to repeat this to yourself or aloud. "I am grateful for...", "I am grateful for...", "I am grateful for...." Continue to repeat what you are grateful for. Allow these words to fill you up.

∞

Hold this gratitude in your heart space. This is the foundation of our practice today. From an energetic perspective, gratitude invites more things into your life for which you can be grateful. Your gratitude is your superpower. Wield it wisely.

∞

With the next few breaths, allow yourself to fully relax. Release any tension that arises in your physical body. Release and relax. You might even say to yourself, "I am relaxed. I release any tension in my body. I soften. I relax."

"I release tension, I soften, I relax."

"I release, I soften, I relax."

∞

I would like for you to look inside your heart and see what you truly desire. What does your heart yearn for? Hold this in your mind's eye. Envision the wanting.

∞

Return to our mantra, "I release any tension, I soften, I relax." Repeat this several times.

∞

Now add to this mantra, "My heart releases the wanting, knowing that what my heart desires is on its way to me."

"My heart releases the wanting, knowing that what I desire is on its way to me."

"My heart releases the wanting, knowing that what I desire is on its way to me."

And again, "I am relaxed. I release any tension, I soften, I relax."

∞

Deep, slow breaths now. Deep, slow breaths. Feel the surface underneath your body. Allow the full weight of your body to be held. You are supported and cared for.

∞

Place your hands on the crown of your head in whatever way feels most comfortable. Take some time here.

"I open myself to receive the bounty of the universe. I am ready."

∞

Begin to slowly open your hands, fingers pointing skyward. "I am receptive. Abundance flows to me. I am ready to receive the gifts that are meant for me."

∞

Return to your posture from the start of our meditation. Hands open and receptive. Breathe deeply, knowing that you have planted the seeds. You will now wait joyfully for all of your dreams to germinate and grow.

"I am open, I am ready, I receive."

∞

Thank yourself for taking this time today. Everything that belongs to you is on its way. You are filled with magic. Namaste.

Affirmation for Today:
I am open and receptive, and everything I want is on its way to me.

The Sixteenth Day

Welcome to your sixteenth day of practice. Let us honor the beauty of this day by greeting the space around us with love. Begin by taking a few slow, deep breaths. Imagine that with each breath, you arrive more fully in this present moment. With each breath, you become more grounded in this space; you become more aware of all that is around you and within you. You expand and deepen with each breath.

∞

What if you could fill a space with love? What if this space, once a series of disparate objects plunked together, suddenly became a unified, interconnected place?

What if you could do this with your mind? Begin to extend your awareness to each item in the space. Furniture, objects, plants, perhaps an animal/pet, or even other people. Bring your awareness to each. Begin to notice the aliveness of each of them. Everything carries a frequency. See if you can recognize the life that swims through everything.

∞

Everything on this planet is made up of the same material. The matter that creates a table is the same matter that creates a plant, a dog, even you. Take time to recognize that these collections of atoms have formed into different shapes, separate from one another, simply by chance. We are all linked; every single thing that exists, and each plant and animal that we meet. We are all made up of the same stuff. It is the matter that matters, and in that matter, we are all one.

∞

Place two fingers on your third eye—the tingly space in the center of your forehead. Take time to connect with this place of intuition, wisdom, connection.

∞

Start to imagine that you are radiating with light. Imagine that this space in the center of your brow is gleaming with light. Notice how it flows all down your body. Notice how it pours out of your brow.

∞

Imagine this light begins to fill up everything and everyone in this space. Take your time here. Every single object and individual sharing this space with you fills with glimmering light.

∞

This light has a name. Let's call it love. It exists exactly as it's meant to. There is nothing different about anything or anyone here. They are all made from the same thing. They are all part of the great oneness. You are made up of the same material. You are exactly perfect, exactly as you're meant to be. There is nothing about anything or anyone in this space that needs alteration, nothing that needs adjustment. There is nothing about you that needs adjustment. You are filled with the light of love that flows through this space. It is beautiful.

∞

Take another slow, deep breath. On your exhale, send gratitude for the energies that exist all around you. You are held and protected by unseen forces. Forces of love, forces of light.

∞

You are connected to all. To everything. To everyone. To yourself. Namaste.

Affirmation for Today:
The light within me sees the light within us all.

The Seventeenth Day

Welcome to day seventeen. How are you feeling today? Let's begin by diving into this query and searching within for the truth here. As you settle into today's practice, adjusting your physical body to arrive fully in this moment, take some time to connect with your experience of the day so far. Is there any residual tension in your body, any trapped energy from the day?

∞

Place your hands on the areas of tension, one at a time, and imagine that your hands have the magical ability to draw this tension out of your body. Breathe slowly and deeply. With each exhale, allow the tension to evacuate your body, and on your inhale, allow the space to fill with love. Tension exits, love enters.

∞

What would it be like to feel completely understood? What if you could fully understand yourself? What if every person you met understood you? How would it feel to be met with understanding any time you start to doubt yourself or feel afraid? What if you were met with understanding when you were angry or upset? How would it feel if every encounter was met with a caring, understanding energy? Take time to feel into that experience. Envision the face of understanding. The voice of understanding. The words they would use. Take time here to feel into this.

∞

I would like you to recall a time when you felt understood. Heard, seen, and truly understood.

∞

How did it make you feel? What was your response to this connection? Try your best not to judge your response. Either then or now. Sometimes we can find connection uncomfortable. That's ok. Be compassionate with yourself, and just investigate. Try not to linger on self-criticism.

∞

What would it feel like if you could validate yourself? In times of uncertainty, what if you could comfort and soothe yourself? What if, in times of fear or confusion, you could look deep within and understand the yearning of your own heart? What if, in moments of humiliation or even shame, you could understand that you were doing your best and know, deep down, that you are still worthy of love and compassion? Give yourself a moment to feel into this.

∞

How would it feel if you could forgive yourself for all the mistakes you've made? Not ignore, not deny, not dissociate from, but accept, and forgive. If you could see yourself just as you are. The entirety of your being. Your experiences, your choices, your energy, your emotions, your thoughts, what if you could see all of you, and love your whole self? How would that feel?

Take some time here to connect with this.

∞

Leaning into our truth is enormously important and impactful for our healing journey. If you cannot look at yourself, flaws and all, and sit with everything you meet, you will never be able to fully heal. Or to fully love yourself. If we can greet the truth of our experience with courage, meet the shame with compassion, and the fear with understanding, we can begin to love our whole selves in a way that is impenetrable, impervious to self-critical thought, and able to stand up to the judgments of others. Our love would become boundless and eternal. Imagine how it might be if we loved ourselves unconditionally. Without the condition of perfection, or the approval of others. Imagine how much space we would have to spread love to others if we could truly love ourselves exactly as we are.

∞

You are understood. You are growing to understand. The truth holds you in love and light. Namaste.

Affirmation for Today:
I am my own support system. I believe in myself. I believe in and honor my story.

The Eighteenth Day

Today is a beautiful day to be alive. Thank you for joining me for our meditation on this glorious day. Find as comfortable a position as you are able, and let's begin by arriving right here, right now. I would like for you to extend particular attention to any tender areas in your physical body.

∞

Is there anything in your body that you are holding and you wish to let go of?

∞

Let's expand this search and begin to look for areas of tenderness in your emotional body. Is there anything particularly raw or sensitive that you are noticing today? Do your best to look with non-judgment. Perhaps you could look at this tender part of yourself as you would look at the suffering of a child. Perhaps you could tend to this place with the same compassion as you would tend to a wounded child.

∞

Take special care not to judge the severity of the tenderness nor to disregard it. Pain and suffering are relative, and it's important that we don't judge our response to our experience. We all have different levels of tolerance, and sometimes those who are the most tolerant of pain are those who are the most disconnected from their experience of it.

∞

It is important to validate yourself. What would you like to hear someone, a loved one, say to you right now? What words would feel helpful for you to receive?

∞

I would now ask you to place your hands on the area where you feel the tenderness most fully and say those words that you would most like to hear. You may say them to yourself or aloud. You can even repeat them, almost as a mantra.

∞

I would like for you to rely on this practice anytime you are feeling lost or helpless. The mantra can change as your needs change.

This is the slow process of learning to understand the deeper parts of ourselves. This is something we can begin to engage in when we are feeling triggered or activated. It can also become something we practice as we scan our bodies in meditation to find tension. This act of tending to our tenderness is a profound way of reconnecting with our wounded inner child. If we can begin to find compassion when everything within us is screaming to judge, demean, or disregard, we are on a beautiful path of self-healing and, ultimately, self-love.

∞

Take some time here to connect with your heart space. You might even place your hands over your heart center. Breathe and imagine this space expanding, filling with warm, loving light.

∞

You are loved. By the universe, by me, and by your future self. Namaste.

Affirmation for Today:
I tend to the wounded spaces inside of me with love and care.

The Nineteenth Day

What would it feel like if you trusted yourself completely? If self-doubt and insecurity played no part in your life? How might your life be different if you could walk with confidence and faith in the direction of your dreams?

∞

Welcome to your practice today. It is an honor to be here with you, connected through time and space.

Let's begin with a mantra: "I am light. I trust this light. I hold this light in my body. This light fills me with vibrant energy. I am light. I am light. I am light."

Repeat this a few times to yourself.

∞

Gently place your hands on your solar plexus, just above your belly button.

Now repeat this mantra: "I am strong. I am resilient."

Say it to yourself or aloud, following at least three cycles of breath.

∞

You are strong and resilient. If you truly knew how strong you were, your doubt would dissipate. If you truly knew how resilient you were, your insecurity would evaporate. You are strong. You are resilient.

When you encounter something challenging, you have the strength to face it head-on. When you stumble, you have the resilience to rise again. And again. And again.

You are strong. You are resilient.

∞

Whenever you are afraid, honor your fear. Be gentle and kind with yourself. Then take a moment to remember how strong you are. How resilient. You have survived everything you have been through thus far.

Breathe into this inner knowledge. Trusting in the truth of your own strength. Trusting in your resilience.

∞

I would like you to try something for me. Trust that it will be ok if I take you on this journey.

Breathe in deeply and slowly. Inhaling trust. Exhaling love.

If you're open to it, take a moment to feel into a moment of fear. When were you last afraid? It could have been something significant or seemingly inconsequential, but really feel into the moment of fear.

∞

If your heart is pumping faster, your nervous system feels activated, and your breathing becomes shallower, I would ask you to return to this present moment and join me for another physical gesture.

If it is available and comfortable for you, hold your opposite arms with your hands across your chest. Your clasp should be firm but gentle.

Breathe into this self-embracing posture and repeat this mantra over the course of five breaths:

"I am brave enough to face this fear. I am strong. I am resilient. I am filled with light.

I am brave enough to face this fear. I am strong. I am resilient. I am filled with light.

I am brave enough to face this fear. I am strong. I am resilient. I am filled with light."

∞

Take a moment to reflect on how it might feel to greet fear with courage.

What might that change about your response to the fear? Would knowing that you are strong enough to handle whatever life throws at you, that you are resilient enough to bounce back from anything, *would knowing that* help you trust yourself enough to greet your fear with courage?

∞

You are a being of light. You have light swirling all around you. It is inside of you. It swirls through every fiber of your being.

You are light. You are light. You are light.

∞

You are a strong, resilient person. Filled with light. And love. Namaste.

Affirmation for Today:
I greet my fear with courage. I can bounce back from anything life throws at me. I am strong. I am resilient.

The Twentieth Day

Welcome to our twentieth day of practice together. Thank you for being here. It means the world to me that we can connect in this way.

Let's take some time here to tune in to our emotional state. How are you feeling? Start to quietly and gently ask yourself how you are. Repeat the question:

"How am I feeling?", "How am I feeling?", "How am I feeling?"

Observe the answer. See what comes up and bear loving witness to it.

∞

Be sure you are not latching onto thoughts. If a thought arises, simply notice it, and continue to ask, "How am I feeling?"

∞

Your thoughts are not your feelings. But many feelings illicit thoughts, especially if these feelings are uncomfortable for us to sit with. Try to feel the feeling. Sit with the feeling, and if a thought arises, recognize that it need not be tethered to this feeling. If you are feeling angry and immediately you start to justify your anger by thinking of all of the injustices you've experienced, then you aren't feeling the anger; you are rationalizing your anger and allowing it to fume. Take time to recognize that the thought and the feeling are separate. It can be challenging at first, especially if we are feeling particularly activated, but the thought and the feeling are not one and the same. They are different. Take time to witness the feeling and then to witness any thoughts that try to link to that feeling.

∞

This is subtle yet enormously powerful work. Each time a thought attempts to grab hold of your emotion and tell you a story about it, you have a choice to allow that automated response to play out or to shift your focus back to the emotion.

This is processing our emotions. *This* is the process.

∞

One of the most incredible things you can learn to do is to bring attention to the system of emotion/thought within you. We all operate using different systems. Yours is programmed specifically for you. You are the only one who can truly, intimately know this system. Know how it works and, more importantly, know how to change it.

Breathe into this knowing.

∞

You are an emotional being. If you continue to ignore your emotions in an attempt to control or change them, you will fail. Our emotions will not be beaten into submission. That is not how this works. You must feel the emotion. There is no easy route, no magic pill. The practice is about inviting awareness into exactly what it is that we're experiencing and sitting with that emotion. Not calling it something, or escaping it, or smushing, smashing, or crushing it, but *feeling* it. We have to feel it.

∞

When we start to *think* our emotions, that's when we become more susceptible to erratic behavior. If, instead, we allow our emotions to express themselves in an integrated way, in a boundaried way, in a safe way, in a way that we choose, then we won't be at the mercy of our emotions. The irony is that we must submit to them in order to master them.

∞

Breathe slowly and deeply. Allowing your whole body to fill with life breath. Place your hands on your low belly and invite a sense of care into your sacral. Imagine an orange light emanating from this space. A brilliant orange light radiating outward, filling your entire body with each breath.

∞

You are an emotional being. You allow your emotions to

speak to you. You allow your emotions to teach you what they are here to teach. Namaste.

Affirmation for Today:
I can hold space for my emotions. I am strong enough to feel them fully. As I walk through the discomfort, I find myself again.

The Twenty-First Day

We have reached the end of our third week of practice. Let's begin today with gratitude. Whatever position you find yourself in, bring to heart one thing for which you are grateful.

Once you have alighted on it, bow your head in a gesture of humble love and appreciation.

∞

Allow yourself to smile. Take a moment here to really smile. This can be an extension of the gratitude you feel. Allowing that gratitude to fill your mouth and pour out through your smile.

∞

If it feels fake or cheesy, that's ok. Invite awareness into the experience of faking a smile. No one is here to call you out on your cheesiness but yourself. So embrace the cheese and smile.

∞

When I say the word "trust" to you, what are the first feelings that flutter to the surface? Take some time to sit with the feelings that the word "trust" elicits.

∞

Do you trust that you will have your basic needs met? Reflect on this for a moment. Do you believe you can trust that your basic human needs will be met?

∞

If any tension, tightness, or heaviness arrives, greet it with compassion. This is foundational work in our root chakra, and while it is vital, the work can be painful if there is a blockage here. You may want to place your hand on your heart space while we reflect.

∞

When we feel that we are not able to trust in our safety and security, when we fear we won't receive what we need for survival, this can create disharmony in our base chakra. Being out of alignment in this space, can lead to anxiety, fear, and anger. You might have a tendency toward overspending or gambling. You could find yourself turning to addiction, creating a further block in your energy field. You may be drawn to home environments that are unstable. You might perpetually find yourself in relationships that are not reciprocal.

The bright side of this dark discovery is that we *can* heal. You have the ability to heal your wounds and begin to trust again, trust more fully than you ever have. When you decide to heal yourself, the healing begins. I know that you are able to open yourself to a more loving, trusting, nurturing life ahead of you.

Breathe deeply and slowly, and allow your breath to embrace you from within.

∞

Feeling that we don't have enough, or we will never have enough, is painfully disempowering. When we experience a limiting belief like this, it is often caused by trauma in the earliest stages of our lives. Healing these ancient wounds takes time, awareness, and a great deal of self-compassion. Let's practice greeting these fears with presence and love.

I would like you to imagine a red flame, warm and comforting, like the hearth after a long day in the cold, ignited in the center of your body at the base of your spine. See this flame flicker and dance.

∞

Breathe in and feed the flames. Breathe out and watch them glimmer.

∞

Right here, right now, in this very moment, is there anything you need? Not want, but need. Is there anything you need at this very moment? Take some time to connect with the word "need." Reflect on the sound of it inside your mind. What does *need* mean to you? Do you need anything right now?

∞

When we ruminate on our basic needs, we often find that we have them all met. We are not starving, we are not dying of thirst, we have shelter, and we have clean air to breathe.

*If you are reading this book, I hope and assume that you are in a safe place, that you have satiated and hydrated your body, and that the air around you is safe to breathe.

If you find yourself in an unsafe environment, if you do not have access to food or clean water, now is the time for you to help yourself. Put all else on hold and care for these essential facts of life. Feed yourself, my darling, find water, find shelter, find clean air, find the safety you deserve.

∞

You are worthy of caring for yourself. We cannot be or do anything effectively if we don't have our basic needs met.

∞

When you begin to look at your basic needs, let's imagine that each one is a brick, a solid, reliable brick. Now, I'm going to ask several questions to help you lay your foundation.

Are you starving?

If not, place a brick on the foundation.

∞

Are you dying of thirst?
If not, lay another brick.

∞

Is the air you are breathing poisonous?
If not, lay another brick.

∞

Do you have shelter?
If so, lay the last brick on the foundation.

∞

Sit here and take in the strength and dependability of this foundation. Breathe into the security of this edifice you are constructing. You are building your fortress. You have the strength to build it. Breathe in, feeling the truth and power of this structure.

∞

What about our emotional needs, which are as important as our physical ones (if not more so)? The process of meeting our emotional needs can be seen as a binder. With each emotional need that is met, we can begin to cement our foundation together—fortifying it.

Let's return now to the word trust. Do you trust that your

basic needs are met? Do you feel a lack? Fear? Uncertainty? If so, hold space for these emotions. It's ok, my friend. It's ok.

Let's take a moment here to focus our attention on what we *do* have. What do you have in your life that is supportive, secure, solid? What in your life makes you feel safe?

∞

What in your life makes you feel supported?

∞

What in your life makes you feel secure?

∞

This is deep healing. I'm proud of you. Please return your attention to the gratitude that initiated this meditation. What are you grateful for now? One thing or many. What are you grateful for?

∞

If it's available, place your hands on your hips and gently but firmly push inward.

Begin to repeat this mantra:

"I am safe. I am secure. I am protected."
"I am safe. I am secure. I am protected."
"I am safe. I am secure. I am protected."

∞

Each time you practice this mantra, you lay cement on the foundation. Each time you acknowledge what you have, you lay a brick on the cement. Each time you practice gratitude, you lay cement on the brick. And so on and so on, building your fortress.

∞

You are safe and secure. You are protected. Namaste.

Affirmation for Today:
I have all that I need. I am grateful for all that I have. I am learning to trust that I have all that I need.

The Twenty-Second Day

Welcome to your twenty-second day of practice. We are entering our final week of practicing together. Let us ground in the power of our growth during these past few weeks. We are stronger, more flexible, more open, and vastly more loving. Seal these aspects into the deepest parts of your being with a slow, deep inhale and a cleansing exhale.

Continue this gentle breathing. You can even chant to yourself,

"I am stronger. I am more flexible. I am more open. I am more loving."

You are a being of Divine Light and Love. Arrive right here, right now. All other thoughts, all other distractions, pale in comparison to this Divine Light that flows through you. Breathe in and feel this light flowing through you. Breathe out and allow this light to float outward, sharing it with the world.

∞

If you were a Divine Being, if that was something you knew to be true. A fact. "I am a Divine Being." Would you act differently? Would you speak differently? Would you make different choices in your life? How would that affect the way you behave?

∞

How might it affect your behavior to know that you are able to shape the world around you? That your actions have a profound effect on others? Would that make you behave any differently?

∞

What if I told you that you had powers you didn't know existed? That your powers enabled you to bring joy and harmony to the world? That they also enabled you to give rise to destruction and discord? How might that impact the way you move through the world? Would you be more cautious with your words? With your actions?

∞

All of this is true. You are Divine. You have the ability to shape the world around you. You have powers you aren't even fully aware of yet. So, how can you create a world that is more peaceful, kinder, and more caring? Let's begin by carving out a space in our minds to create this loving world.

Imagine a door in the center of your mind. Beyond this

door is a room. It is peaceful, calm, and comfortable. Open the door and walk into the room.

∞

You may begin to fill this room with things that are pleasing to you. Take a moment here to build the furnishings of the room. What physically exists within this chamber?

∞

The room is safe and comfortable. Everything here is exactly what you would like it to be.

Connect with your sense of smell. Where is the beautiful smell in this room coming from? Is there a candle burning that provides a warming scent? A bouquet of aromatic flowers on a windowsill? Or is there something in the room itself? A cozy, familiar scent that feels like home? Whatever the smell is, sense into it. Discover the aroma here.

∞

How is the temperature so pleasant in here? Is there a window open, allowing a gentle breeze to drift in? Is there a hearth keeping the room warm and inviting? Feel the temperature of the room.

∞

What sounds can you hear within this peaceful room? A crackling fire? Music playing in the corner? A dog snoring? A cat purring? A friend chatting? A loved one laughing? A lazy brook babbling outside the window? What is that peaceful sound? Where does it come from? Discover the sounds in this room.

∞

You are here, in this space, surrounded by love and light. Here you can begin to create. Take a few slow breaths here, and arrive fully in this beautiful room.

∞

You have the ability to control every aspect of this room. So let's begin to create. How would you like to feel in this room? You can fill it with anything, joy, peace, contentment, hope, connection, support, empowerment, confidence, worthiness, love.

Fill this room.

∞

When anyone enters this room, they fill up with the feelings you have created here. Who would you like to invite into this room right now? It can be anyone in the entire world. Living or passed on. You can even invite a pet into this room. Anyone. Or no one. But whoever they are, they cannot change the feelings this room elicits.

This is a magical room, after all.

∞

You can always ask someone to leave as well. Sometimes

we want someone in our room; sometimes, we don't. And that's ok.

∞

How does it make you feel to know that you control every aspect of this space? You control who comes in, who goes out, when they leave, what's in here, and how it smells, feels, and sounds. You can create anything you want in this perfect room. Breathe into this feeling.

∞

You have the ability to create your own reality. In your mind, you can reach a place of clarity that allows for further doors to open and other rooms to be discovered and explored. You have such power here.

∞

We can manifest what we want to summon into our lives. Here lies the groundwork for developing this skill. We must first cultivate a deep understanding of our wants, what we like and dislike, what makes us feel loved, and what makes us feel isolated. We must create this foundation, and the first step is self-inquiry.

∞

You can stay in this room for as long as you want. You may return to this room as often as you'd like. Chances are, you will have to update this room as you evolve and grow. Feel free to make any alterations you see fit.

This is your space. Here, you are free.

∞

You are free to build the life of your dreams. Namaste.

Affirmation for Today:
Divinity flows through me. I live the life I've imagined.

The Twenty-Third Day

Welcome to your twenty-third day of practice. Honoring yourself by arriving here and now is the most significant gift you can give. Being present. With your energy, your emotions, your thoughts, and your feelings. Engaging in daily mindfulness is vital for connecting with our inner wisdom. Vital for our health. What you are doing is recalibrating your patterns on a cellular level. Unlearning and relearning. Breaking and building. It is such exceedingly important work. Critical work.

Let's begin.

I would like for you to take a few very slow breaths to begin today. As slow as you can comfortably take.

∞

With each inhale, imagine a cool current of water flowing through your body. Clearing and cleansing any stagnant energy.

On your exhale, imagine all those blockages pouring out of your body—an exodus of unwanted energy.

Repeat this cycle until you feel ready to move on.

∞

You are buzzing with life. Every cell in your body is alive. Take a moment here to really feel into this truth.

"I am fully alive. Every fiber of my being is teeming with life."

From your crown to your toes. From your shoulders to your fingertips, your navel to your knees. You are alive. Bask in your aliveness.

∞

I would like for you to bring your attention to your heart space. Gently ask yourself if there is anything you need. Anything your heart is asking for at this moment.

∞

If I asked you to nurture yourself, what comes to mind? If I asked you to care for yourself, how would you begin? Take some time here to connect with your natural reaction to nurturing, and be present with whatever you find. Try your best not to judge your reaction. Simply invite a loving presence.

∞

What if you could nurture yourself by validating your own experience? How would it feel if you were on your own team? Would that feel different for you? What if you were rooting for yourself? Might that affect your daily mindset? Take some time to feel into the exquisite power and care of self-validation.

∞

What if right here, right now, you are enough? What if there is nothing that you have to do, say, be, think, feel, or create in order to be enough? What if you, just as you are, are exactly who you need to be? What if you are enough?

∞

Inside, there are all kinds of mechanisms at work to keep you healthy and safe. Your body works so hard just to make sure you're protected and comfortable.

The tricky part is that your body began this regulation process when you were young. So, there may be areas that were perceived as threats that are no longer dangerous for you. There also may be ways in which your body learned to regulate itself that aren't serving you now. Would you ever allow a child to make decisions for you? Probably not. We don't have to allow this underdeveloped system to reign over our experience. We can do things differently. What would it feel like if you were at the helm? How might it be different if you were the one calling the shots? Determining what is a threat and what isn't. Deciding how you are going to respond to the real threats.

Take a moment to feel into this.

∞

The other difficult aspect is that sometimes perceived threats can trigger the same response as actual threats. When we project our minds into the future, our imaginations can go wild, detecting potential threats all over the place. It's important to bring intentionality to our lives. Deciding what is important for us and what is not. Then we can decide whether we want to listen to our younger selves or not. We can choose to maintain protection around those aspects that feel tender. We can also choose to release the security systems around aspects that we only perceive to be threatening. Our bodies don't want us to feel afraid, but fear is a wonderful and powerful device when harnessed properly. We can use our fear to teach us where our boundaries are. We can also commune with our fear and see if there are things it has always tried to protect us from that might not be so bad. Vulnerability is a scary thing, but it is one of the most critical practices we can engage in. If we didn't do things we were afraid of, we would never challenge ourselves, never try anything new, never meet new people, never travel. Never know the excruciating joy of vulnerability.

∞

Let's breathe together, knowing that you are breaking through heretofore unknown blockages that have been keeping you small. Safe, but small. Breathe slowly and try to release any tension as you exhale.

∞

You are supported by your body, your mind, your whole self. Namaste.

Affirmation for Today:
I listen to my fear, and I choose my response. I honor my feelings, and I choose my life.

The Twenty-Fourth Day

Welcome to your twenty-fourth day of practice.

Imagine, if you will, a brilliant burgundy light emanating from the bowl at the base of your torso. As you inhale, it glimmers. As you exhale, it swirls and swims throughout your body. Inhale and it glows. Exhale and it expands. After your seventh breath cycle, it has fully filled your entire body with this glimmering deep red light.

∞

If you're open to it, I would like for you to clasp your hands together, interlocking your fingers. Now raise both of your middle fingers, touching one another, creating a steeple, of sorts, with your hands.

Imagine all of the deep red light that was swirling throughout your body has poured into your hands, and is radiating outward between the cracks in your fingers.

∞

Breathe slowly and deeply, and with each inhale, watch the light shine brighter still, and with each exhale, watch that light slowly shine outward - sharing this light with the world.

Take three rounds of breath, and on your final breath, imagine that the light is all around you. Floating through the air, enveloping you in brilliant, warm light.

∞

Release your hands, and place them on your heart space. You are filled with love and beauty. There is so much healing you have done, so much compassion in your heart, so much you have to give, and so much yet to receive. Trust in the power of your own growth. You are expanding. You are ascending. I am so honored to be part of your journey.

∞

You are grounded in your own goodness. You are secure, safe, and protected. Namaste.

Affirmation for Today:
I am a being of light and love. I have roots that sink down into the earth and ground me here and now.

The Twenty-Fifth Day

Welcome to your practice today. No matter where you are, what you're doing, or what state you found yourself in when you arrived here today, take a moment to thank yourself for being here. Sometimes the most challenging aspect of self-improvement is showing up. The hardest step you'll ever take is the first one. So, well done. You're here. You're doing something many people don't, believing in yourself enough to be here.

∞

Let's imagine for a moment that you are a vessel. You are not a compilation of thoughts and feelings but rather a carrier that holds the essence of you within it.

∞

I'd like to take you on a journey today. Let's shed the skin of this mortal form and rise out of our physical bodies. Floating gently above yourself. From here, start to explore the room you're in. Take time to investigate. Soar, hover, fly.

∞

For the next 10 to 20 minutes, I will grant you a very special gift. You will be able to transport yourself anywhere in the world, anytime in the world. You get to decide where you will go and when that will be. You could visit your childhood home, the park near your school, that tree you used to climb, or your favorite spot on the beach. Where and whenever you'd like to travel, you are able to do so now.

There are only two rules. The first is that you must have been to this place in your lifetime. The second is that this must be a place of joy for you. A place that brings peace and happiness to your soul.

∞

Now that you have chosen a destination take some time to fully arrive. What is this space filled with? What does the air smell like? Take some time to familiarize yourself with this place. You can float through the air or drift, but you are formless, the self without the body. Explore this space now.

∞

Who is in the space? Are there people here? Are you alone? Take a moment to recognize all the people who have been here, honor any of the animals that may have roamed this place. Connect with the energy that lingers from the other individuals who have wandered here. We are all connected in this vast expanse of consciousness.

∞

Is there someone you would like to be with here? It could be anyone. Is there any person, passed or with us, who you would like to join you in this place?

I grant them access to arrive here with you now.

∞

They are formless, floating beings. You can feel their presence, hear their voices, but rather than arriving as the form, they are the essence of the person. Take time to connect with them.

∞

What would you like for them to say to you? What would you like to say to them? Or would you simply like to bask in the light of their presence? You decide.

∞

I want you to be present with them. Take this time to observe, in quiet gratitude, the simple beauty of this joyful place. Allow the harmony of gratitude to brighten your being. Then, watch as this light fills those who accompany you.

Take as long as you'd like with this.

∞

Who are you without the physical form you typically

inhabit? Who is this *you* inside of you? Who is this *you* that exists without connection to the physical form?

∞

You are.

That is all. You are. You exist. What a wonder. You are. And that is enough.

∞

We will now journey back home. Wherever you are, you may begin to float through time and space, returning to the here and now.

Check in with yourself. How are you feeling? After your sojourn, do you feel rested, joyful, relaxed? Or do you want more?

Connect with your experience here.

∞

You may return to this place as often as you like. We are slowly building a world where you are free from your daily toils. Take time to be present with anything you're moving through with loving kindness.

∞

You are the formless taking form. You are a vessel filled with Source energy, and you are Source energy filling a vessel. Namaste.

Affirmation for Today:
__I am the Divine in human form.__

The Twenty-Sixth Day

Welcome to your practice today. For this meditation, we will be connecting very deeply with our senses. As always, I ask you to find as comfortable a position as possible. Once you've done that, let us begin.

Take three slow, deep breath cycles to arrive right here, right now. With each inhale, follow the sensation of the breath entering your body. With each exhale, track your breath as it leaves your body.

∞

Begin to invite curiosity about the smells in the room around you. Can you detect any aromas? What are they? How do they make you feel?

If nothing is coming up for you, hold your palms in front of your face and inhale. This can stimulate your olfactory, so you can more easily detect other scents.

If still nothing presents itself to you, simply breathe slowly and deeply. Sometimes if we continue our breathing with the awareness of scent, we will begin to notice different smells.

∞

Now, imagine your favorite smell. It can be a general smell like lavender, or it could be very specific, like "the way my backyard smells after the rain."

Really connect with the smell that brings you joy, peace, or relaxation.

∞

Just allow yourself to bear witness. You don't need to do this in any particular way. You don't need to be "good" at these observations. Arriving here with the intention of connecting with our senses on a deeper level is the most important thing.

Take a moment to look around you. Wherever you are, take some time to observe the space. What are three things that stand out to you?

∞

How does this place make you feel? Does it elicit any emotions? Connect with the feelings that come up as you look around this space.

∞

Let's take a few more deep, rejuvenating breaths together. Coming back into our bodies.

∞

I now invite you to close your eyes and connect with

sound. We will begin by listening to the sounds that are loudest, closest, and most dominant. What do you hear? Gently close your eyes, and listen.

∞

I would like for you to extend this awareness to any deeper, more distant sounds. Are there any sounds that are maybe a level quieter than the first group? Try to connect with these sounds now. This might take a few moments of awareness and concentration, but really try to discover what's here.

∞

I would like for you to do this once again, this time attempting to notice the sounds that are farthest away, the deepest, most subtle sounds you can hear. Can you do this for me? Try to really connect with the sounds that are underneath the noise. This will take longer still than the other two, but really try to hear more than your ears are accustomed to.

∞

Wonderful. Now we're going to connect with touch. As a Reiki Practitioner, this is essential for me. Connecting and reconnecting and connecting again with touch is vitally important for my work.

So, let's begin by sensing the feeling of the air on your skin.

∞

How about the feeling of your body? What is here right

now? Does your stomach feel empty? Are your muscles sore? Is your body tight? Do you feel tingles or vibrations anywhere? Really feel into what's here.

∞

Let's gently invite some physical touch. If it's available to you, take one of your hands and slowly, with great gentleness, begin to rub down the opposite arm, starting at the shoulder and moving down to your hand.

This kind of thing might feel silly or uncomfortable if you're not accustomed to receiving nurturing energy. However, if you practice, you will slowly become more comfortable with nurturing, and eventually, it can be a wonderful self-regulating process.

∞

Now move on to the other arm. With the opposite hand, gently move down your arm from the shoulder to the hand very slowly and with great tenderness.

∞

How are you feeling? Do you feel more relaxed? More at peace? Connect with any sensations that have arisen since you began this practice today.

∞

Let's take a few more of those slow, deep breaths together.

∞

Today, I have a homework assignment for you. At your next meal, I would like for you to eat without any distractions. No phone, no tv, no podcasts. With each bite, I want you to chew slowly and intentionally. I want you to notice every flavor that hits your tongue. I want you to be aware of how the flavor makes you feel.

∞

You are a deeply feeling person. You are a wide expanse of sensations teaching you how you respond to the world around you. Namaste.

Affirmation for Today:
I am waking up. I am rising.

The Twenty-Seventh Day

Welcome to today's meditation. With each practice, you become wiser, stronger, and more buoyant. I am so proud of you for the work you are putting in.

In today's practice, I would like you to have something to write with and something to write on.

Let's begin.

We are focusing on developing and strengthening your intuition today. Take a moment to imagine that the inside of your head is filled with glittering indigo light. It's swirling and swimming all throughout your mind.

∞

Let's imagine that on your next inhale, this light glows brighter, and on your exhale, it begins to float out of the center of your forehead. Inhale, and it glows brighter, exhale, and it floats outward. Repeat this for three breath cycles. On the final inhale, it shines as bright as the sun, and on this final exhale, all of this light floats out of your third eye into the air around you.

∞

You are connected to everyone and everything. Your intuition is always available to you. All we need to do is trust in the power of our connection. As Source sails into you, your intuition then takes hold of this energy and comprehends it on a deeper level. If you practice engaging in intuitive practices, your intuition will grow stronger and stronger.

First, we have to start with a relatively clean slate. Let's take a moment to simply be here together. How are you feeling? Are you experiencing any physical tension? Are there any sore areas in your physical form? How is your vessel feeling today?

∞

What about your emotions? How are you feeling emotionally? Is there any tenderness you are evading? Any soft areas that need some attention? How is your mood? Do you feel balanced? Calm? Overwhelmed? Take some time to feel into whatever exists in your emotions today.

∞

If you are experiencing any intense emotions, let's see if there's any way that we can process these feelings in order to arrive here from a more aligned place. Do you need to do a brain dump? Just write down everything in your mind, all your to-dos and distractions, to get them out of your head and onto a reliable piece of paper.

Would you like to call a trusted friend? Someone who is kind and supportive, who doesn't make you feel judged? Would you like to move your body? Take a walk, dance, work out, or shake your limbs to shift that energy? Do you need to emote? Have a good cry or a laugh? Do you need some comforting self-touch, gently rubbing your opposite arms (continuing the practice from yesterday), giving yourself a hand massage, placing your hands on your heart space, or on your feet?

Take some time to connect with what you need to feel more balanced right here and now.

∞

If you are feeling particularly triggered, or you need extra time, please remain here, processing. This is enormously important. You can pick up from this point at a later time.

Now that you have taken time to process any emotions that need your attention, we will continue.

Gently close your eyes, and begin to connect with your intuitive mind. We will start small here. Remember, intuition is about trusting and releasing. Do not hold tight to any response you receive. Simply trust the answer, and let it go.

If there is any one question in your life right now that you are most interested in seeking more clarity on, invite that question into your consciousness, and begin to ask it. You can almost chant this question. Repeating it in tandem with your breath cycle. It might sound something like this "I would like more clarity on my relationship with _____. What do I need to know to help me find peace with them?" or "What do I need to do in order to make my work more resonant?" Ask this question 5 times, and on the fifth time, open your eyes, and write down whatever comes to mind.

Try your best not to judge. Trust the process, and then let it go.

∞

You can always return to this practice. It is important to do these kinds of exercises often in order to connect more deeply with your intuition. Like your muscles, your intuition needs regular exercise in order to maintain its optimal functionality.

I would like for you to close your eyes once again and bring someone you love to mind. The first person your mind lands on is the one you should choose.

∞

Take some time to hold this person in your awareness. How do they look? How do they feel? Do they seem happy? Sad? Angry? Hurt? Calm? Doubtful? Curious? Tired? Energized? Embarrassed? Content? How do they seem as you view them with your inner vision?

∞

I would like for you to feel into the sensation of receiving a warm, comforting hug. What does that feel like? Really try to feel that support and love.

∞

Imagine that the sensation of a hug transforms into a glimmering warm light. On your next exhale, I would like for you to send this light to that person who came to mind. It can travel through time and space, so send it as far as you need in order for them to receive it.

∞

If possible, you might consider reaching out to this person today. If that's not possible, simply write down your findings.

You may discover that this person had you in their thoughts as well or that you were tapping into a particularly powerful energy that they were giving off.

Let's take three slow breath cycles together. Connecting more deeply to our inner life with each breath.

∞

You are connected to every being on this planet. And to yourself. Namaste.

Affirmation for Today:
I use my intuition to further my connection with the world around me. I am an intuitive person, and I spread love and light through my inner wisdom.

The Twenty-Eighth Day

Welcome to practice. This is the final day of our final week, but not to worry, we have two more meditations together. Soon you will be engaging in this practice on your own. Now that we have tread this path alongside one another with courage and strength, I am very excited for you to begin carving your own path.

Let's begin.

I want to take a moment to connect with the word "strength." See what arises for you with this word.

We will begin by asking a few questions about strength. Try not to judge your responses; simply listen to them and notice any of your unconscious beliefs that arise. You are a wonderful person, and there is no reason to invite shame here. Move forward from here with love.

∞

Strength. Are there any images that float to the surface of your consciousness when you are holding this word? If so, take a moment with those images. How do they make you feel? Protected? Safe? Maybe afraid? Perhaps incapable? Maybe excited? What comes up for you?

∞

Do you see yourself in the images? Is there a part of you (or perhaps more than a part) that feels connected to these images of strength?

∞

Do you feel strong? Do you see yourself as a strong person?

∞

What would it take for you to feel strong? What are the qualifications for strength in your mind?

∞

Is it possible that those qualifications are an inaccurate barometer of strength?

On the other hand, they might be an incredibly efficient way to measure strength. Just take a moment to mull over this question.

∞

If you see these credentials as accurate, then try to find ways in which your actions align with those words. For example, if you chose "courageous," ask yourself where in your life you exhibit courage. I personally think it's pretty courageous to take on a 30-day meditation challenge. Even if you haven't followed day by day, taking time to try something new, something probably a little intimidating, taking time to improve yourself is very courageous!

So, take some time to find ways in which you display these attributes of strength.

∞

Along those same lines, if I were to tell you that you are strong. That I know you are strong. That I know you have great strength, a vast well of strength deep within you that you have yet to tap. How would you feel?

If I were to ask you to name the ways in which you are strong. If I were to ask, when do you demonstrate strength, and how do you display this strength? How would you respond? Take some time to recall your moments of strength.

∞

It can be difficult for many of us to feel strong. At times it can feel so evasive that we find it hard to believe we've ever been strong. But human beings are strong by nature. We are the ones who survive. When we take our first breath, we are daring to exist. When we take our first steps, we are courageously going where we've never gone before. We are incredible!

∞

Accountability is enormously significant in practicing strength. We have to recognize that everything in our lives is our responsibility. It might not be our fault, but it is our job to do something about it. As part of our strength practice, we have to practice accountability. It is one of the scariest things you can do, which means it provides the greatest potential for tapping into our strength.

"Well, if I say I'm wrong, won't others judge me? Blame me? Ridicule me? Stop liking me?"

To move forward in truth and to take responsibility for our actions, acknowledging the impact we have on others, is one of the strongest things we can do. Courage is being afraid and doing it anyway. Strength is being uncertain and still taking that first step into the unknown. When we hold ourselves accountable for our actions and words, and for the impact we have on others, we are practicing one of our greatest strengths.

∞

When we start to lose confidence in ourselves, we can be tempted to allow the thoughts, feelings, beliefs, and projections of others to tarnish our own understanding of our deep strength.

If I told you that you are strong, courageous, and confident, that you have great fortitude and power, would you start to recognize the parts of you that are confident? That are powerful? That are truly strong?

∞

Life force energy, think about those words… Life. Force. Energy. Life force energy flows through you. You are filled with this powerful energy. All you need do is harness it, bring intentionality and focus to it, and trust it. It is always, *always* there. Always supporting you, filling you up. Breathing your breath, pumping your blood. You are alive. Against all odds, and the strength that takes is unfathomable.

∞

Strength is not always about brawn. One of the strongest aspects of humans is our ability to be vulnerable. It might sound counter-intuitive, but our vulnerability is our greatest strength. Courage cannot exist without fear, and without vulnerability, we cannot be truly strong.

Let's re-examine the images that came to mind earlier. Are these images of burliness, of great feats?

What if the images of strength could be a bit more subtle? What if strength is the first conversation about something you are struggling with? What if strength is taking the next steps after loss, loss of a job, a relationship, or a loved one? What if strength is finally laughing again after great heartache? What if strength is choosing truth over comfort? What if it's standing beside the ridiculed? What if it's believing in yourself after a disappointment? What if it's still loving yourself after someone criticizes you? Strength is a state of being. You are strong. You do strong things every single day. Nearly every moment. If you find it hard to trust your strength, perhaps return to this meditation more often in your upcoming practice.

∞

Repeat after me in your mind or aloud for three breath cycles, "Every moment, I can choose strength, and I grow stronger."

Breathe slowly and deeply. Feel the air flood your body with life force energy.

∞

Be kind to yourself today. It is vitally important that you develop a gentleness for yourself as we practice introducing a deep trust in your inner power.

∞

You deserve to celebrate your strength. Namaste.

Affirmation for Today:
I am growing stronger daily, and I am strong today.

The Twenty-Ninth Day

Speak with truth. Only with truth. Practice speaking only with truth today.

This is the second to last day of our 30-Day Challenge. Our penultimate meditation. I will have some homework for you, but before we get into that, let's begin with some healing breathwork.

Take a few moments to really ground yourself. Whether seated, lying down, or standing, take some time to connect with the ground beneath you. Recognize that you are being held and supported. Root into the felt sense of security, and take slow, deep, measured breaths. You might even invite silence into your breathwork. This is about connecting internally to a sense of stillness and calm.

∞

Let's play around with vocalization. When we connect with our throat chakra, it's not just about communication. It's also about conscious thought and using our authentic voice. It's about honesty and truth.

To begin with, we'll focus on the muscles that help us to connect our internal and external lives. The voice is what allows our insights and intuition to shift from within to without. So, take a moment here to breathe in and on your exhale, open your mouth, and allow whatever sound is available to you to burst forth for the entire length of your out-breath.

∞

You can play around with this if you're not familiar with vocal exercises. Perhaps let out that breath on a "sssss" sound. You could try "vvvvv" or "shhhhh" or "gaaaaa."

You could try the Bija or "seed" Mantras: "Lam," "Vam," "Ram," "Yam," "Ham," and "Om."

Take some time here to fill your lungs with oxygen, and on your exhale, allow your breath to release through whatever shape your lips are compelled to make.

Repeat this for seven breath cycles.

∞

For today, I would ask you to do two things. The first might be very difficult, and it is not about perfection. Here it is: Speak with truth. Only allow truthful words to pass your lips today.

This is a practice of recognizing the difference between

truth and untruth in our words, our actions, and our lives. Do not allow your fear to dictate your conviction.

The other stipulation is to be kind. Just be kind. Recognize the impact you have on others.

Many of us are taught that connection is about gossip or complaining about others. So, true connection can feel elusive for us. If we practice only letting kind and true words pass our lips, we can begin to forge genuine relationships.

This practice of only speaking with truth and kindness could mean that you spend a great deal of the day in silence. So today, let's practice trusting that silence is not something to be feared. If we allow it, silence can be a space where we develop the kind of patience required for a richer connection with our truth, ourselves, and each other.

It is tremendously difficult to change our patterns of behavior. They didn't arrive overnight, and they won't depart overnight either. Others in your life will have a hard time with the change. They will. If you expect this to be an easy, graceful, elegant egress from your unaligned life to a life of balance and alignment, you are going to be disappointed. It will be uncomfortable. Others will push back. You will feel awkward and probably alone. That is unless you are blessed with open-minded, loving, and aligned friends already. And if that is the case, you should feel grateful every day because that is uncommonly rare.

Take time to remember the importance of truth. What is important about truth for you? What is the value of truth in your life?

∞

Why do you think we hide from the truth? In what ways have you hidden from it? And why did you hide?

∞

We have to return to accountability here. We are all responsible for ourselves. So often, when we are practicing self-love, we ignore the part we play in some of our pain and suffering. It can be tempting to believe that others are responsible for your pain. And sometimes, tragically, that is true. But sometimes, it's not, and it is your responsibility to determine the difference. You have to rise and take the helm. You must steer your own ship. We, humans, do not need to constantly oscillate between opposite poles. But rather, we can hold both strength and vulnerability, accountability and self-love, truth and kindness within us.

Everything is a blend of the black and the white with which we desire to paint the world. The gray area becomes illuminated by our acceptance of this complexity. We are the shimmering silver light that emerges from the integration of the two. We can be healing and still wounded, honest, and still tell lies. We can make mistakes and still be worthy of love. And if we have all of these apparent contradictions swimming inside of us, it doesn't mean there is something wrong with us. It means that we are human.

∞

I'd like to touch on trust for a moment. Like so much

of what we cover in this book, trustworthiness is a practice. When we are integrated, and what we say aligns with what we feel and believe, this is one way that we are able to practice being trustworthy. When we say we will do something and we do it, this is another way of being accountable. When we hold the privacy of others as a sacred understanding, in other words, when we don't gossip or share secrets that don't belong to us, we are moving toward integrity.

If you are unaccustomed to this kind of alignment, then it doesn't happen overnight. It requires diligence, but rest assured that if you integrate your words, actions, and thoughts, you can cultivate healthy, open, trusting relationships with yourself and each other.

∞

You are an honest, open, and thoughtful person.

Affirmation for Today:
Today, I speak the truth. Today, I speak with kindness.

The Thirtieth Day

On behalf of my wisest, most empowered, and aligned self, guide my words, my thoughts, and my actions today in loving comfort and perfect balance. Help me practice self-compassion, bring more peace and understanding to the world, and invite more empathy into my relationships with others. Help me make the world a better, brighter place.

Welcome to your final day of practice with me. I am enormously proud of the work you have done to get here. You have shown such resilience and fortitude, and in order to continue this beautiful work, those qualities are going to be immensely helpful.

Today will be all about recognizing your achievements, acknowledging where you still need some attention, and celebrating the beauty of this balance. You have come so far. You have so far to go. Yet, you are here, in the center of your journey, exactly where you need to be, precisely where you are meant to be. You are moving towards deeper love and acceptance and moving away from the tendencies that have held you back. I hope you are as proud of yourself as I am of you.

For today's meditation, I would like for you to deeply connect with your own practice. Our focus today is "Loving All of You." We have dipped our toes into mindfulness meditations, breathwork meditations, astral projection meditations, body scanning, affirmations, Reiki meditations, and many more. I would like you to begin by mentally flipping through our previous meditations and bringing to mind one of them that you particularly resonated with. You don't need to recall the entire session, just a part you felt connected to.

Take some time to reflect.

∞

As we gently move through our final meditation together, I would like you to really connect with what feels best for you. Thinking back on these thirty days, have there been aspects of these meditations that you've been more excited about than others? This is very useful inventory to clock. Take time to trust your body as it tells you what it most yearns for.

∞

After reading this passage, I want you to close your eyes and picture your future self. It can be fifty years in the future or five. However far into the future they are, make sure they represent your favorite self. They have everything you want now, and they have an ease, a grace, a joy about them that is undeniable and comforting.

SELF LOVED | 135

Take time to find your favorite future self. Gaze upon them, really take them in.

∞

I would like for you to ask them a question, it can be any question. Take a moment to look them in the eyes, and ask the question you most want answered. Then, and this is important, trust whatever answer you receive.

It may not make sense now, but it will. In time.

∞

I would like for you to reach out your hand and place it on their heart. They will accept your touch gratefully and slowly extend their own hand to place it on your heart. As they do this, a cord will form between you. This sacred gesture will link your current self to your future self, binding you together in harmony and love.

∞

You can take a few more moments to connect with this place, with your future self, and with your current self. Acknowledging that you are never stuck, you are always moving forward.

∞

Every single day you have choices that can either bring you closer to the person you want to be or pull you farther from your favorite self. I urge you to be aware that every single decision you make is one of those choices. Honoring your wants and needs, inviting compassion for yourself and others, taking accountability for your actions and your energy, and trusting your own reactions to the impact others have on you. All of these practices can help you move toward your most aligned self. Trust the process, trust the practice, honor the life-giving energy that flows through and around you.

∞

You are filled with the love of the universe and the love of yourself. I love you. Namaste, my friend.

Affirmation for Today:
I am on a path to becoming my favorite self, and I love myself every step of the way.

The Author

Anna Fable is a level III Usui Reiki master practitioner, meditation teacher, and writer. She's helped hundreds of thousands of people heal themselves and learn present-moment living. She believes in the power of mindfulness, suffused with compassion and acceptance, to change not only the course of our lives but our entire world.

She creates free healing sessions for the collective on her YouTube Channel, YouTube.com/ReikiwithAnna.

Cover Art
Lisa Taranchenko

Milton Keynes UK
Ingram Content Group UK Ltd.
UKHW020954221123
433051UK00021B/1230